the final week

the last eyewitness:

Illustrated by Rob Pepper

by chris seay and david capes

world
PUBLISHING
SINCE 1928

Published by World Publishing, Inc.
Nashville, TN 37214
www.worldpublishing.com

Design and layout by
Scott Lee Designs | www.scottleedesigns.com

Printed in the United States of America

1 2 3 4 5 6 7 8 9—14 13 12 11 10 09 08 07 06

Contributors

The Last Eyewitness: the final week

Illustrated by: Rob Pepper
Commentary essay written by
Chris Seay and
David Capes

Scriptures retold from *the* voice
A Scripture project to rediscover the story of the Bible

Retold by:
Matthew: Lauren Winner
Mark: Greg Garrett
Luke: Brian McLaren
John: Chris Seay
Daniel: David Capes

Scholarly review by:
Darrell Bock
David Capes
Alan Culpepper
Peter Davids
Felisi Sorgwe
Jack Wisdom

Editorial review by:
Maleah Bell
James F. Couch, Jr.
Amanda Haley
Kelly Hall
Holly Perry
Ramona Richards

Acknowledgments

Kelly Hall, your tireless and passionate work on this book is greatly appreciated.

Alan Culpepper, your teaching on this book a decade ago has inspired my deep love for this narrative. It is an honor to have you help in telling the story accurately.

David Capes, I am so grateful to be working closely with you on this project.

Frank Couch, your passion to see the Bible come to life in beauty and truth has sustained us through the many challenges that arise.

Greg Garrett, your help is invaluable to me.

The good people at **World Publishing**, I am blessed by your enthusiasm and commitment to this project.

Ecclesia, as a church we have embodied these things together. I love you all!

Emergent, **BGCT**, and **A29**, thank you for the many ways you have blessed the journey this book represents.

Lisa, my four beautiful kids, my siblings, and **parents**, I am more committed than ever in my love for all of you.

Carrying the Cross

As I have contemplated the last week in the life of Christ as told by the beloved disciple, I have mourned the reality that my friend Kyle Lake has spent his last week on this earth. Kyle was a pastor, thinker, father, husband, son, brother, and faithful friend. His absence has left a void in the lives of his family, those in the University Baptist Church of Waco, Texas, and his friends in the Emerging Church conversation. This book is dedicated to UBC and the Lake family. May they find the strength to live out the gospel in the way of the disciples, celebrating life and the love of God in the face of tremendous grief and loss.

Table of Contents

Preface

The Last Eyewitness: the final week is the work of a community of believers who, though they don't live in close community, share the bond of a passion for the spirit and vitality of the Scriptures. It is this passion for the beauty and richness of the story of God's redemptive history that inspires this work. Our desire is that you would enter into the drama of the last week in the life of our Savior as the apostle John brings it to life. This is the greatest story ever told.

To keep the focus on the story, special emphasis has been given to Christ's teaching and the dialogue that John uses so effectively. Alongside John's narrative, portions of the other three Gospels have been included to fill out the story. A simple note at the bottom of each page indicates which chapter that Scripture portion is from. Also, whenever there is a break for an illustration or comment the passage that follows is identified. Also, unique insights from scholarly sources have been written as if John were sharing them to his followers and have been placed within a thin gold border to distinguish them from Scripture. At times the text of Scripture has been expanded to clarify a passage. These few elaborations are in italic type. An index at the end of this volume lists every Scripture reference. Also, the story behind **The Voice** Scripture project is told in the Epilogue. Scholars, a poet, a novelist, preachers, writers, editors, and an acclaimed artist have all given their considerable talents to bring the week of Christ's passion alive. Our desire is that God touches you with this most intriguing narrative. Join with us in rediscovering the story of the last week in Christ's life.

Beloved

beloved witness:
you've cast your net
drawn us in.
our bodies soaked of sin,
hang by the fire to dry
where we crowd, His children
    before your tired feet,
        once washed by the God-Servant,
           toes caked in mission dust.

there, you tell, re-tell–
of the last burst of blood
    scattered upon stone skin
how you turned with running cries
    as love slept, three long days before...
        life-freedom rose over mourning as the Son
how your belief opened
    as an awakened eye
        framed through holes in holy hands.

will we enter into your struggle?
    know your inability to shake away:
        forever-hope
found in the pinnacles of His eye-stars.

our spirit hands grab words by fistfuls
to stain-press them into paper
hoping they would be so much more than red...
    but heard, felt, touched; lived–

you held the Man of our dreams!
heard stories of creation read from His palms–
    bellied true fullness at breakfast on the beach
    found honest comfort,
        leaned into His love-chest.

His voice, still rattles your old man bones
    curled, and aching for an eternity
        that comes only
           through His promise fulfilled.

Kelly Hall

Chapter 1

Making a Beginning

In the beginning... there was no written word.

*R*ight about now, I can hear you thinking, "What?" But it's true. I am sure during your life you have either thought or heard someone say, "In the beginning was the Word," in reference to the Bible. Have you ever seen a pastor hold up his Bible and say, "In the beginning was the Word"? I have; and it confused me. I hope someone took the time to explain to you (as they did for me) that *logos* (which is often translated as "word") is actually a metaphor for Jesus. This insight helped me, but only gave me a partial truth. I then associated Jesus with a written word. To me, this meant He was passive, stale, mundane, and static. In actuality the Greek word *logos* is anything but passive. It is the perfect word for John and his community to express the ultimate significance of Jesus. To the Greeks the *logos* was the creative and unifying principle of the cosmos. For centuries their philosophers and leaders had speculated on what power or substance held everything together and gave humans the ability to understand and relate to the world. They called this mysterious, wonderful entity the *logos*. To the Jews, however, the *logos* had a more personal aspect. In their Scriptures the refrain "the word (*logos*) of the Lord came to the prophet" set the rhythm of past revelations and future expectations. In this sense the *logos* is God's voice speaking, echoing through history. It is His word, His message, His communiqué. But they understood that God's Voice revealed more than God's will; it also revealed God's glory and God's true self. The word "voice" provides us with an excellent way to express this transcendent reality. It is active, powerful, truthful, and full of the energy of life. *Logos* or "voice" is the personification of all that is wise and good.

Much like the beginning of the universe, God's journey as a man began with speech, and continues to be propelled into the human consciousness as we retell it to one another. The beginning was about hearing, not reading.

I love the way John, a beloved disciple of the Messiah, begins his narrative of the origin of life:

> Before time itself was measured, the Voice was speaking.
> The Voice was and is God.
> This celestial Voice remained ever present with the Creator;
> His speech shaped the entire cosmos.
> Immersed in the practice of creating, all things that exist
> were birthed in Him.
> His breath filled all things with a living, breathing light,
> Light that thrives in the depths of darkness,
> blazing through murky bottoms.
> It cannot, and will not, be quenched (1:1-5).

For hundreds of years no one had heard His voice, there had been no word from God. The ancient prophecies lay in the dust and waited. Generations lived and died wondering whether the "Voice" from heaven would be heard again in their day. Century after century, the faithful remnant of God's Sinai covenant lived under

oppressive regimes: Assyria, Babylon, Persia, Greece, and Rome.
Prophets are born in crisis and exile. They mourn for a day of
justice and peace in midst of chaos. They see the future, not in
crystal clarity, but in broad strokes of promise and fulfillment.
At the perfect time, the future envisioned by Israel's seers began
to take root in the ancestral lands of Israel. One oracle, spoken by
Isaiah of Jerusalem, promised that those living in darkness would
see a great light. Zebulun and Naphtali, the northernmost reaches
of the promised land, were destined to experience the first
glimmers of that new, creative light. This was only just, for it was
these villages and towns that fell first to Assyrian aggression in
Isaiah's day. So the Voice came into the world and settled in Galilee. Clothed in flesh, the Light of the World shined in the darkness.

Nearly 2,000 years ago on the eastern edge of the Roman
Empire, a Galilean carpenter, Jesus of Nazareth, was baptized
by John the Immerser, in the Jordan River. Jesus saw a vision of
the opening of heaven and heard His Father's voice declare His
divine Sonship. As the voice of the Father thundered through the
heavens Jesus knew it was time to leave behind Nazareth and His
earthly father's trade to take up a new calling. He gathered together a small company of followers in Galilee and settled in Caper-
naum. He told them that God's rule was breaking into the world
and that those who wanted to be on the right side of God's favor
should change their ways and heed His teachings.

As He traveled the countryside, unsuspecting spectators were
healed, and the crowds celebrated the popularity of this carpenter turned prophet, hoping to be liberated from the oppression of
Rome. Some hailed Him as the Messiah, God's agent whom the
prophecies said would arise to bring justice, peace, and an end
to Israel's exile. Eventually His actions caught the attention of
the powers-that-be in the empire. Some were convinced He was
a dangerous subversive who threatened their nation, way of life,

John the Apostle

the last eyewitness: the final week

and ancestral faith, while others claimed He was in league with the devil himself. For a time He avoided their attempts to discredit Him publicly and silence His voice.

This is the story of the very last week in the earthly life of Jesus. His entire ministry came down to these last seven days. It was a week that would rock the entire world and humankind from that point forward. Out of the betrayal, trial, suffering, execution, and resurrection of Jesus came a movement of believers. These followers of the Crucified One shook the children of Abraham and altered society forever. This story is told by the one known as the "beloved disciple."

Tradition tells us that the beloved disciple took Mary, the mother of Jesus, into his own family. They moved from the land of promise to western Asia Minor (modern Turkey near Izmir). The name "John" often appears in the record during and after this time. There is John the evangelist, John the apostle, John the elder, John the son of Zebedee, John of Patmos, and "the beloved disciple." Do all these refer to the same person? We can't be certain. Many stories circulate around this noble and saintly figure from the past. Some happened. Some did not. Again we can't be certain. But there is an especially resilient tradition that locates John the apostle in and around Ephesus in the last decades of the first Christian century. He lived, apparently, to a ripe old age, well beyond the normal span of life. He gathered around him a group of witnesses to whom he told and retold the inside story of his experience with Jesus. His accounts inspired them to pull together the memoirs of the beloved disciple—the last eyewitness to the life of Jesus—and wrote them down so others would also know and believe.

When all the other disciples had paid for their faith with their lives, and John approached the end of his days, the community of the beloved disciple recorded the events of the Savior's ministry. The account in this book only covers the final week in Christ's life. A background commentary that runs throughout this book is provided as a first person aside, as if it were written by John. The purpose is to draw the reader into the characters and the events of the story. We often read these passages quickly and give little attention to the emotions and details of the events. In this book we hope to slow the pace just a bit so we can hear the voice of John, the last eyewitness, at the end of his life. The story is his and we are his audience.

John's Gospel was born on an island known as Patmos to where he was banished. If you know the way God works, you realize that being deported, banished, captured, jailed, or enslaved is just another way of saying that you are being sent by God on a missionary journey. That's how God orchestrates the spread of His redemptive narrative. This was the case with the beloved disciple: a man enters a new land and culture, looks around, takes a deep breath, and starts a church.

I grant you, the church did not have a steeple, pulpit, baptistry, finance committee, or a parking lot. But have no doubt; this was a church in the truest sense—a Christ-filled community with celebrations and dinner parties, shared finances, house meetings, and habitual gatherings on the beach around the fire. John would sit nearest to the fire, and the community would collect themselves around him to listen and ask questions. I can only imagine the kind of questions they asked him about Jesus, the gospel, and God's activity in their own lives:

Did Jesus like spicy foods?
Did He like His fish grilled or blackened?
Did He say if He ever had a fistfight with His brothers?
Did He shave His neck, or let His beard grow down low?
How often did He bathe?
Did He think cleanliness was next to godliness?

Why didn't He overthrow His opposition and become king?
Do you remember Him ever getting sick or having a headache?
Why did He ask you to care for His mother?
How many hours did He typically sleep in a night?

In many ways the Gospel of John is so different because questions like these and the people who asked the questions shaped it. John spoke the story of Jesus Christ in beautiful detail and prose. Thankfully, John and his community of believers eventually put pen to papyrus to ensure that the story would be retold perpetually until Christ returns to live out the sequel. This narrative record that we know as the "Gospel of John," closes with an insightful apology:

> There are so many other things that Jesus said and did, if these accounts were also written down, the details would be so vast that the number of books could not be contained in the entire cosmos (21:25).

This epilogue is the announcement of a deep regret that there is not enough paper or trees or library space available to tell you the whole story—an admission that spoken words have served us well and the written word is limited, incomplete, and restrictive. Yet, here you are, reading the written word, you carry a Bible chocked full of written words, and you often believe the written word. The Bible is the source about the beginning, although it's not the beginning. The Bible is a witness to the true Word of God that was with God in the beginning. But let's not put the cart before the horse. This story is interactive. If you are going to really hear this story, you need to activate your imagination and allow your heart to absorb the power in the reality of Christ speaking directly to you today. Throughout *The Last Eyewitness* you will come upon illustrations by Rob Pepper. Each of these is an interpretation of a recognized work by a master artist. Rob's illustrations are an outflowing of the work of the Holy Spirit. With each illustration, he created his interpretation by a method he calls *conscious reflex drawing*. You will find a description of this unique process in the Epilogue. Rob trusted the Spirit to bring new life to a treasured masterpiece.

The Voice, Jesus Christ, did not just speak in A.D. 30 or in A.D. 95, about the time the Fourth Gospel was written; He is speaking into your life right now. So come into the story, smell the mixture of the salty air and billows of smoke floating from the bonfire and hear the Last Eyewitness…

Chapter 2

Learning to Serve

My name is John. My father's name was Zebedee. We made our living by fishing on the Sea of Galilee. I am the last eyewitness to the life of Jesus. All the rest are gone, some long gone. Many died years ago, tragically young, the victims of Roman cruelty and persecution. For some reason Jesus chose me to live to be an old man. In fact, some in my community have taken to calling me "the elder." I suppose that's because there are others with the name "John" in our community.

I am the inspiration behind the Fourth Gospel. These are my stories, recorded, told to you by my disciples. I'm proud of what they have done. Me? I've never done much writing. But the story is truly mine.

You see my hands. They've been hurting for the past 20 years now. I couldn't hold a pen even if I wanted to. Not that I was ever good at writing. I was a fisherman so my hands were calloused. I could tie ropes, mend nets, and pull the oars, but never make a decent *xi* (Greek letter). So we used secretaries when we wanted to write. There was always a bright young man around it seems, ready to take a letter or help us put pen to papyrus. Even our brother Paul used secretaries—Tertius, Luke, and Titus—just to name a few.

John the Evangelist

My eyes are too weak to read anymore. I can't remember the last time I could see well enough to read a letter or even see the inscriptions. So one of the brothers (I call them, "my little children") read to me. They are all very gracious to me in my old age, compiling my stories, bringing me food, laughing at my jokes, and caring for my most intimate needs. Time is taking its toll on me though. I rarely have the energy to tell the old stories and preach entire sermons. Instead, I simply remind them of Christ's most vital command, saying as loudly as I can, "Little children, love one another." I repeat this phrase quite often.

Jesus had this group of guys. He called us "the twelve." We traveled with Him, spent time with Him, ate with Him, and listened to Him talk about God's kingdom. We watched Him perform miracles. These weren't the tricks like you see in the market or attempts at magic you hear about at shrines. These were what I call signs. Something was breaking into our darkness. These signs pointed to a greater reality most people didn't even know was there. In the other Gospels they call them miracles or works of power. We've decided to tell you about select signs because these, more than any, revealed the true glory of this Man.

Jesus wanted us to be His family, a different kind of community. We figured it out later. By calling us "the twelve," Jesus was creating a new people of God. God was doing something new, like the prophets had promised. We were living at the center of history. From now on everything would be different. This made us feel special, proud, and sometimes arrogant. We'd sometimes jockey for Jesus' attention. Even within "the twelve" some were closer to Jesus. He had this "inner circle" of sorts. I was part of it. Peter, Andrew, James, and I were with Jesus at times when the other fellows had to stay behind. I'm not sure why He picked me. Because of that, I knew He loved me and I would have a special place with Him.

Jesus also had other students. Not all of them stayed. Some came and some went. I don't really know how many people in all. One time He sent out seventy of us to proclaim the good news and heal in His name. He even let women be His students. Most people don't know this, but women were among those who helped support us financially (Lk 8). At a time when people said it was a shame for a man to be supported by women, Jesus took their help and took it gladly. For Him it was like a badge of honor. But there were no women among "the twelve." That was only right. In our day women didn't travel with men who were not family. Scandal was always swirling around Jesus; He didn't want or need to fight that battle.

I've outlived all the rest of "the twelve" and His other followers. I can't tell you how lonely it is to be the last person with a memory, some would even say a fuzzy memory, of what Jesus looked like, the sound of His voice, the manner of His walk, the penetrating look in His eyes. All I can do is tell my story.

The Scripture says God knows the length of our days. Jesus reminded us that the Eternal has the hairs of our head numbered and knows when a little bird drops from the sky. So He knows how this feeble body aches. The mornings are the worst times.

I used to sleep—one of the benefits of a clean conscience, I suppose. But I don't sleep much anymore. Now these memories fill my thoughts. I constantly think about all those experiences of being with Jesus each day. So at night I think, I remember, I pray, I wait. I still look for His coming.

Some brothers have criticized me for my hope in His coming. They say that this is all that there is. What we have, of course, is great—the Spirit is strong with us, we have a vibrant community, God does things among us no one can explain—but still, I know there is more. I've seen it in His eyes. Oh, there's so much more.

So I wait.

Others criticize me for neglecting the blessed hope of His coming. I can't win. Because I speak so passionately of God's blessings now and how the Kingdom is with us now, some accuse me of forgetting about His coming. Nothing could be further from the truth.

Those of us who walked with Jesus were like most Jews in my village. We expected the Messiah to field an army, face off with the Romans, and reestablish the glory days of David and Solomon. We were completely disarmed by the simplicity and power of Jesus' voice, of His message. Only after the resurrection did the full weight settle in of what He said.

Before Jesus came along, many thought John the Immerser might be the Messiah. But when Jesus appeared in the wilderness, John pointed us to Him. The Immerser knew his place in God's redemptive plan. But there are still those who think he was more significant than Jesus. That movement is especially vocal in Ephesus. I feel like it is important for me to set the record straight. John the Immerser was a man sent from God. But Jesus is the Voice of God. John rejected any messianic claim outright. Jesus, though, accepted it with a smile, but only from a few of us—at least at first. Don't get me wrong, John was important, but he wasn't the Messiah. He preached repentance. He told us we were flawed—seriously flawed and we needed God's help. So he told everybody to get ready for One greater to come along. The One who comes will immerse us in fire and power, he said. John even told some of his followers to leave him and go follow Jesus.

Others have written accounts of what happened among us. I'd like to hear what they all have had to say. The ones I have heard have done a good job. But I have stories to tell no one is talking about. The other Gospels have faithfully portrayed the public Jesus. But I feel compelled to tell the story of the private Jesus. The others show us how Jesus preached and dealt with the multitudes. But I still remember the small group time with Jesus and the conversations that Jesus had with Nicodemus, the Samaritan woman, and the man born blind—I don't remember his name.

The other Gospels tell the tragedy and injustice of Jesus' death. Here was the single greatest man in history who was falsely accused; who was dragged before corrupt priests and a cruel Roman governor. He was condemned to death and crucified in a most hideous manner. On a human level, Jesus' arrest, condemnation, and crucifixion was a tragedy of epic proportions. But the more this old man thinks about what happened, the more I understand now that Jesus' death was His greatest hour. Things seemed to spin out of control so quickly. One minute we were celebrating the Passover together in the upper room; the next we were running for our lives! I'm not sure who was to blame for what happened to Jesus. Envious priests. The Roman governor. But, in fact, He was in complete control. That's why I say the hour of His death was the hour of His greatest glory. That's why I think that when Jesus was lifted up on the cross, He became the means by which all people can come to God. The most vivid memory that lingers in this old man's mind is of Jesus up there, on the cross. I can still see it like it was yesterday. His body—hanging halfway between heaven and earth, embracing the world—bridged the gap between God and humanity.

But I am getting way ahead of myself. There is one part of this fascinating story that I want to tell you about right now. Of all the things this old man has seen in his many years, the things that we saw and heard that week were the most startling.

Now I want to be very clear. This is my story, but unlike what you hear from most storytellers, this is completely true. I am giving you the testimony of an eyewitness. And like my brother disciples, I will swear upon my life that it is true.

John 13

¹Before the Passover festival began, Jesus was keenly aware that His hour had come to depart from this world and to return to the Father. From beginning to end, Jesus' days were marked by His love for His people. ²Before Jesus and His disciples gathered for dinner, the adversary filled Judas Iscariot's heart with plans of deceit and betrayal. ³Jesus, knowing that He had come from God and was going away to God, ⁴stood up from dinner and removed His outer garments. He then wrapped Himself in a towel, ⁵poured water in a basin, and began to wash the feet of the disciples, drying them with His towel.

Simon Peter | 6 *(as Jesus approaches)* Lord, are You going to wash my feet?

Jesus | 7 Peter, you don't realize what I am doing, but you will understand later.

Peter | 8 You will not wash my feet, now or ever!

I have to interrupt the story so you can get the whole picture. Can you imagine what it would feel like to have Jesus (the creative force behind the entire cosmos) wash your feet?

Have you ever been in a gathering where a rich and powerful person offers to fill your glass? You are thinking, "I should do this myself. How is it that someone of your stature would be willing to serve me?" But later you find yourself serving those who would view you as rich and powerful in the same ways that you were

Jesus Washing the Disciples' Feet

served. Multiply that experience by thousands, and you will have a small glimpse of this powerful expression.

My life changed that day; there was a new clarity about how I was supposed to live. I saw the world in a totally new way. The dirt, grime, sin, pain, rebellion, and torment around me were no longer an impediment to the spiritual path—it was the path.

Where I saw pain and filth, I found an opportunity to extend God's kingdom through an expression of love, humility, and service. This simple act is a metaphor for the lens that Christ gives us to see the cosmos. He sees the people, the world He created—which He loves—He sees the filth, the corruption in the world that torments us. His mission is to cleanse those whom He loves from the horrors that torment them. This is His redemptive work with feet, families, disease, famine, and our hearts.

So many of you have missed the heart of the gospel and Christ's example. When you see sin exposed in people, you shake your head and think how sad it is. Or worse you look down at these people for their rejection of God, lack of understanding, and poor morals. This is not the way of Christ. When Christ saw disease, He saw the opportunity to heal. Where He saw sin, He saw a chance to forgive and redeem. When He saw dirty feet, He saw a chance to wash them.

What do you see when you wander through the market, along the streets, on the beaches, and through the slums? Are you disgusted? Or do you seize the opportunity to expand God's reign of love in the cosmos? This is what Jesus did. The places we avoid, Jesus seeks. Now I must digress to tell a bit of the story from long before. I remember Him leading our little group of disciples into one of the most wretched places I have ever seen. It was a series of pools where the crippled and diseased would gather in hopes of being healed. The stench was unbearable, and no sane person would march into an area littered with wretched bodies and communicable diseases. We followed Him reluctantly as He approached a crippled man on his mat and said to him, "Are you here in this place hoping to be healed?" The disabled man responded, "Kind Sir, I wait, like all of these people for the waters to stir, but I cannot walk. If I am to be healed by the waters, some-one must carry me into the pool. So, the answer to Your question is yes—but I cannot be healed here unless someone will help me. Without a helping hand, someone else beats me to the water each time it is stirred." So, Jesus said, "Stand up, carry your mat and walk." At the moment Jesus uttered these words a healing energy coursed through the man and returned life to his limbs—he stood and walked for the first time in thirty-eight years (5:6-9).

It was not clear to us whether or not this man deserved this miracle. In fact, many of the disciples were disgusted by his lack of gratefulness and that he implicated Jesus to some of the Jewish authorities for healing him on the Sabbath. But God's grace is not earned; it is a beautiful gift to all of us.

When Jesus washed our feet He made an announcement to all who follow His path that life would not be about comfort, health, prosperity, and selfish pursuit.

I have gotten away from the story that was barely started. Let me back up and start almost from the beginning of the story again.

John 13

Simon Peter	6	*(as Jesus approaches)* Lord, are You going to wash my feet?
Jesus	7	Peter, you don't realize what I am doing, but you will understand later.
Peter	8	You will not wash my feet, now or ever!

Jesus		If I don't wash you, you will have nothing to do with Me.
Peter	9	Then wash me but don't stop with my feet. Cleanse my hands and head as well.
Jesus	10	Listen, anyone who has bathed is clean all over except for the feet. But I tell you this, not all of you are clean.

¹¹He knew the one with plans of betraying Him, which is why He said, "not all of you are clean." ¹²After washing their feet and picking up His garments, He reclined at the table again.

Jesus		Do you understand what I have done to you?
	13	You call Me Teacher and Lord, and truly, that is
	14	who I am. So, if your Lord and Teacher washes your feet, then you should wash one another's
	15	feet. I am your example, keep doing what I do.
	16	I tell you the truth: an apostle is not greater than the master. Those who are sent are not greater
	17	than the One who sends them. If you know these things, and if you put them into practice,
	18	you will find happiness. I am not speaking about all of you. I know whom I have chosen, but let the Scripture be fulfilled that says, "The very same man who eats My bread with Me, will
	19	stab Me in the back." Assuredly, I tell you these truths before they happen, so that when it all
	20	transpires you will believe that I am. I tell you the truth: anyone who accepts the ones I send accepts Me. In turn, the ones who accept Me, also accept the One who sent Me.

²¹Jesus was becoming visibly distressed.

Jesus	I tell you the truth: one of you will betray Me.

²²The disciples began to stare at one another, wondering who was the unfaithful disciple. ²³One disciple in particular, who was loved by Jesus, reclined next to Him at the table. ²⁴Peter motioned to the disciple at Jesus' side.

Peter		*(to the beloved disciple)* Find out who the betrayer is.
Beloved Disciple	25	*(leaning in to Jesus)* Lord, who is it?
Jesus	26	I will dip a piece of bread in My cup and give it to the one who will betray Me.

He dipped one piece in the cup and gave it to Judas, the son of Simon Iscariot. ²⁷After this occurred, Satan entered into Judas.

Jesus	*(to Judas)* Make haste, and do what you are going to do.

²⁸No one understood Jesus' instructions to Judas. ²⁹Because Judas carried the money, some thought he was being instructed to buy the necessary items for the feast, or give some money to the poor. ³⁰So Judas took his piece of bread and departed into the night.

³¹Upon Judas' departure, Jesus spoke:

Jesus	32	Now the Son of Man will be glorified as God is glorified in Him. If God's glory is in Him, His glory is also in God. The moment of this astounding

	33	glory is imminent. My children, My time here is brief. You will be searching for Me, and as I told the Jews, "You cannot go where I am going."
	34	So, I give you a new command: Love each other deeply and fully. Remember the ways that I have loved you, and demonstrate your love for
	35	others in those same ways. Everyone will know you as followers of Christ if you demonstrate your love to others.
Simon Peter	36	Lord, where are You going?
Jesus		Peter, you cannot come with Me now, but later you will join Me.
Peter	37	Why can't I go now? I'll give my life for You!
Jesus	38	Will you really give your life for Me? I tell you the truth: you will deny Me three times before the rooster crows.

Ultimately, Peter was telling the truth. He was more than willing to lay down his life. But none of us understood the magnitude of the persecution and hatred that was about to be unleashed on all of us. You ask me, "Did that change the way you led and treated people in your community or outside of it? Some of us think you have an ax to grind with the Jews. What connection did this pattern of living have with Jesus' command to love? How can you reconcile your angst against the Jews and this command Christ gave you to love?"

Chapter 3

Learning to Love

So you noticed I had a few things to say about the Jews. It took me awhile to figure out why you all seem to cringe every time the subject arises. I have decided that people are overly sensitive when we make generalizations about a group of people. But remember, I am a son of Abraham, as are many in my community. I am not slandering a people. When I talk about "the Jews," I am talking about a corrupt group of power brokers who conspired against Jesus with the Romans to have Him crucified and later had my people expelled from the synagogue. They are members of my family. I do not hate them. I only hate what some of them have said and done to the followers of Jesus. I am no more anti-Jewish than Micah, Isaiah, or Amos. Prophets who speak for God criticize hypocrisy and unbelief and stand for justice. I am just following the example of the prophets.

Our community has helped me pull together some essential Christian teachings to make this clear. In these letters I specifically say, "If you say you love God, and hate your brother, you are a liar" (1 Jo 4:20). So if you use my teaching as justification to hate anyone, then you are missing the point.

Jesus made it clear to us that following His path is all about loving one another. Some of these people are hard to love, I admit it. They attacked Jesus for healing the lame man by the pool and almost everything else He did, and now they are persecuting all of us who follow Him. But, this is one of our greatest honors—to be mistreated for His sake. My friend Matthew often reminded us of Jesus' teaching to love our enemies. It isn't easy to love our enemies, but it is even more challenging sometimes to love the people we live with.

If you want to have an apologetic for faith, the apologetic is love. And the challenge of it for us—as many of you have figured out—is that you can't fake it. Love is one thing you can't manufacture. You might be able to pull it off for a little while; you might even have behavior that is of a loving nature. But love, real love, always flows from something deeper. It flows from Christ.

Christ came into this world saying, "What I'm here to do, is to teach you how to love, but I have to demonstrate it." It was so important to demonstrate His message that He came to live among us so that we could begin to grasp what was going on.

He makes it very clear in His final words that we must not only live by the Ten Commandments but also by this great commandment to love God and to love our neighbor. And Jesus could have gone on and reviewed it all—He knew it all—but He didn't go into any of it. What He chose to make clear before He left was this: "If you want to be one of My followers, it's going to be marked by a posture and demonstration of love, and in fact, that kind of love will be judged according to the way I love, which is loving up unto the point of death."

Part of love is serving one another. Allowing others to serve you is as important as serving others. So you honestly want to know, "What is it like as an old man letting others serve me?"

I hate it. I enjoyed sharing love with others through service, my sermons, and kind deeds. Now everyone is taking care of me. But it is a blessing to the community. One must give and receive.

In the later years of life you spend more time receiving.

All of us who walked with our Lord were startled by His emphasis on service. Everything He did, all His thoughts were from a life given in service. He called each of us to serve one another as He had served us. Luke heard it a little differently than I did, but He wrote about this same evening and how Jesus challenged us to follow Him and to serve.

Luke 22

²⁰And similarly, after the meal had been eaten He took the cup.

Jesus		This cup, which is poured out for you, is the
	21	new covenant, made in My blood. But even
		now, the hand of My betrayer is with Me on this
	22	table. As it has been determined, the Son of
		Man, *that firstfruit of a new generation of*
		humanity, must be betrayed, but how pitiful it
		will be for the person who betrays Him.

²³They immediately began questioning each other:

Disciples	Which one of us could do such a horrible thing?

²⁴Soon they found themselves arguing about the opposite question:

Disciples		Which one of us is the most faithful, the most
		important?
Jesus	25	*(interrupting them)* The authority figures of the
		Gentiles play this game, flexing their muscles in

The Lord's Supper

competition for power over one another, masking their quest for domination behind words like 'benefactor' or 'public servant.' But you must not indulge in this charade. Instead, among you, the greatest must become like the youngest and

27 the leader must become a true servant. Who is greater right here as we eat this meal—those of us who sit at the table, or those who serve us? Doesn't everyone normally assume those who are served are greater than those who serve? But consider My role among you. I have been with you as a servant.

28 You have stood beside Me faithfully

29 through My trials. I give you a kingdom, just as

30 the Father has given Me a kingdom. You will eat and drink at My table in My kingdom, and you will have authority over the twelve tribes of Israel.

31 Simon, Simon, how Satan has pursued you, that he might make you part of his harvest.

32 But I have prayed for you. I have prayed that your faith will hold firm and that you will recover from your failure and become a source of strength for your brothers here.

Peter 33 *Lord, what are you talking about?* I'm going all the way to the end with You—to prison, to execution—*I'm prepared to do anything for You.*

Jesus 34 No, Peter, the truth is that before the rooster crows at dawn, you will have denied that you even know Me, not just once, but three times.

We all struggled with the fear of what was going to happen once Jesus was gone. Every day we woke up eager to listen to Christ's teachings and to journey with Him on unknown adventures. Following Christ makes sense when you can see Him, but how do you follow something or someone you cannot see? When He was gone, who was going to lead? We had grown accustomed to looking the Creator of the heavens and earth in the eyes each day; the prospect of something more abstract seemed like a setback. We were scared, naturally, as Jesus laid out before us the future events. Remember how I told you what Jesus said:

John 13

Jesus 31 Now the Son of Man will be glorified as God is
32 glorified in Him. If God's glory is in Him, His glory is also in God. The moment of this astounding
33 glory is imminent. My children, My time here is brief. You will be searching for Me, and as I told the Jews, "You cannot go where I am going."
34 So, I give you a new command: Love each other deeply and fully. Remember the ways that I have loved you, and demonstrate your love for
35 others in those same ways. Everyone will know you as followers of Christ if you demonstrate your love to others.

Simon Peter 36 Lord, where are You going?

Jesus Peter, you cannot come with Me now, but later you will join Me.

Even Peter, dear Peter was afraid. He protested any inference to Jesus' impending departure. We all would have done the same. Jesus assured us and tried to keep us connected, "I am the vine and you are all branches" (15:5). He calmed our fears over and over again with stories, metaphors, and outright promises saying, "I would never abandon you like orphans. I will return to be with you" (14:18).

The key to being a disciple of Jesus, to being like those of us who were with Him from the beginning, is found in the instructions that He gave to prepare us for His physical exit from the cosmos. No one could have imagined that in Christ's absence we would become stronger, more diverse, and more intimately connected with Jesus than ever before. In His absence we gained three new sources of strength that cannot be underestimated: the Holy Spirit, the church, and hope of our eternal home with the Father. He gave us real hope.

John 14

Jesus

1 Don't get lost in despair; believe in God and
2 keep on believing in Me. My Father's home is designed to accommodate all of you. If there were not room for everyone, I would have told you that. I am going to make arrangements for
3 your arrival. I will be there to personally greet you and welcome you home, where we will be
4 together. You know where I am going and how to get there.

Thomas

5 Lord, we don't know where You are going, how can we know the path?

Jesus

6 I am the path, the truth, and the energy of life.

No one comes to the Father except through Me.

7 If you know Me, you know the Father. Rest assured now, you know Him and have seen Him.

Philip 8 Lord, all I am asking is that You show us the Father.

Jesus 9 *(to Philip)* I have lived with you all this time and you still don't know who I am? If you have seen Me, you have seen the Father. How can

10 you keep asking to see the Father? Don't you believe Me when I say I abide in the Father and the Father dwells in Me? I'm not making this up as I go along. The Father has given Me these truths that I have been speaking to you, and He

11 empowers all My actions. Accept these truths: I am in the Father and the Father is in Me. If you have trouble believing based on My words,

12 believe because of the things I have done. I tell you the truth: whoever believes in Me will be able to do what I have done, but they will do even greater things, because I will return to

13 be with the Father. Whatever you ask for in My name, I will do it so that the Father will get glory

14 from the Son. *Let Me say it again:* if you ask for

15 anything in My name, I will do it. If you love Me,

16 obey the commandments I have given you. I will ask the Father to send you another Helper, the

17 Spirit of truth, who will remain constantly with you. The world does not recognize the Spirit of truth, because it does not know the Spirit and is unable to receive Him. But you do know the Spirit because He lives with you, and He

18 will dwell in you. I will never abandon you like
19 orphans; I will return to be with you. In a little
while, the world will not see Me, but I will not
vanish completely from your sight. Because I
20 live, you will also live. At that time you will know
21 that I am in the Father, you are in Me, and I am
in you. The one who loves Me will do the things
I have commanded. My Father loves everyone
who loves Me, and I will love you and reveal My
heart, will, and nature to you.

The Other Judas **22** Lord, why will You reveal Yourself to us, but not
to the world?

Jesus **23** Anyone who loves Me will listen to My voice and
obey. The Father will love him, and We will draw
close to him and make a dwelling place within
24 him. The one who does not love Me ignores My
message, which is not from Me, but from the
Father who sent Me.

25 I have spoken these words while I am
26 here with you. The Father is sending a great
Helper, the Holy Spirit, in My name to teach
you everything and to remind you of all I have
27 said to you. My peace is the legacy I leave to
you. I don't give gifts like those of this world.
28 Do not let your heart be troubled or fearful. You
were listening when I said, "I will go away, but I
will also return to be with you." If you love Me,
celebrate the fact that I am going to be with
the Father because He is far greater than I am.
29 I have told you all these things in advance so
that your faith will grow as these things come

30 to pass. I am almost finished speaking to you. The one who rules the world is stepping forward

31 and he has no part in Me, but to demonstrate to the cosmos My love for the Father, I will do just as He commands. Stand up. It is time for us to leave this place.

The Holy Spirit brought the teachings of our Lord right out of the world and into our very beings. God would now dwell in the hearts of all true believers, and the chasm between God and man would be destroyed. As you can imagine, the idea of Jesus leaving created a whirlwind of fear and doubt for us. I say whirlwind, but it was more like the equivalent of staring down a volcano. But once again, Jesus reached in gently and calmed our storms when He said, "I will now dwell inside of you." A reconnection is made between God and us, much like the first days in the garden—God the Creator strolling in paradise with Adam. God is, once again in Jesus and the Holy Spirit, present amid suffering, hope, sin, and friendship.

Chapter 4

Living in a Vineyard

At a time when all of us were feeling as if we were about to be uprooted, Jesus sketched out a picture for us of this new life as a flourishing vineyard. A labyrinth of vines and strong branches steeped in rich soil. Abundant grapes hanging from their vines ripening in the sun. Jesus sculpted out a new garden of Eden in our imaginations—one that was bustling with fruit, sustenance, and satisfying aromas. This is the kingdom life. It is all about connection, sustenance, and beauty. Jesus said to us, "I am the vine, and you are the branches. If you abide in Me and I in you, you will bear great fruit. Without Me, you will accomplish nothing. If anyone does not abide in Me, he is like a branch that is tossed out and shrivels up, and is later gathered to be tossed into the fire to burn. If you abide in Me and My voice abides in you, anything you ask will come to pass for you. Your abundant growth and your faithfulness as My followers will bring glory to the Father" (15:5-8).

The Holy Spirit is our nourishment in cold winds and withering heat. It connects us to Christ and the Father through all seasons. So, lay down any fear you have about being disconnected from God—the Creator of the Universe dwells within you, sustains you, and will accomplish the impossible through you.

We, the church, take on our role after Jesus' exit as the incarnate Christ, and we become His body here on earth. The vineyard not only reminds us that we are intimately connected to the living God, but it also reminds us that our journey is to be shared in community. Throughout history, the church has brought together men, women, and children, and created a family of sisters and brothers, bridging all races, nationalities, and ideologies.

The church is the redeeming force in the world. If you are to know Christ you must know His body. From almost the very beginning it has been said *extra ecclesiam nulla salus*, "outside the church there is no salvation." A life in Christ is not just about embracing and loving God; it's about being a living branch on the vine. The body of the church—the vineyard—calls us to embrace one another finding strength, passion, and comfort in our collective mission.

John 15

Jesus

1 I am the true vine, and My Father is the keeper
2 of the vineyard. My Father examines every branch in Me and cuts away those who do not bear fruit. He leaves those bearing fruit and carefully prunes them so that they will bear more
3 fruit; already, you are clean because you have
4 heard My voice. Abide in Me, and I will abide in you. A branch cannot bear fruit if it is disconnected from the vine, and neither will you if you are not connected to Me.
5 I am the vine, and you are the branches. If you abide in Me and I in you, you will bear great
6 fruit. Without Me, you will accomplish nothing. If anyone does not abide in Me, he is like a branch that is tossed out and shrivels up, and is
7 later gathered to be tossed into the fire to burn.

The Vine and Branches

If you abide in Me and My voice abides in you,
8 anything you ask will come to pass for you. Your abundant growth and your faithfulness as My followers will bring glory to the Father.

9 I have loved you as the Father has loved Me.
10 Abide in My love. Follow My example in obeying the Father's commandments and receiving His love. If you obey My commandments, you will
11 stay in My love. I want you to know the delight I experience, to find ultimate satisfaction, which is why I am telling you all of this.

12 My commandment to you is this: love
13 others as I have loved you. There is no greater way to love than to give your life for your friends.
14 You celebrate our friendship if you obey this
15 command. I don't call you servants any longer; servants don't know what the master is do-ing, but I have told you everything the Father
16 has said to Me. I call you friends. You did not choose Me. I chose you, and I orchestrated all of this so that you would be sent out and bear great and perpetual fruit. As you do this, anything you ask the Father in My name will be
17 done. This is My command to you: love one another.

18 If you find that the world despises you, remember that before it despised you, it first
19 despised Me. If you were a product of the world order, then it would love you. But you are not a product of the world because I have taken you out of it, and it despises you for that very
20 reason. Don't forget what I have spoken to you: "a servant is not superior to the master." If I was

mistreated, you should expect nothing less. If they accepted what I have spoken, they will also

21 hear you. Everything they do to you they will do on My account because they do not know the

22 One who has sent Me. If I had not spoken within their hearing, they would not be guilty of sin, but now they have no excuse for ignoring My voice.

23 If someone despises Me, he also despis-

24 es My Father. If I had not demonstrated things for them that have never been done, they would not be guilty of sin. But the reality is they have stared Me in the face, and they have despised

25 Me and the Father nonetheless. Yet, their law, which says, "They despised Me without any cause," has again been proven true.

26 I will send a great Helper to you from the Father, one known as the Spirit of truth. He comes from the Father and will point to the truth

27 as it concerns Me. But you will also point others to the truth about My identity, because you have journeyed with Me since this all began.

As Jesus warns us of the mistreatment we can expect, He disarms our fears by reminding us of the most important things. If the Spirit is in us, we have no reason to fear man. In fact, the church often thrives under persecution, not prominence. Yet, we are obsessed with power and political prominence as a means to influence the culture. It seems that the world of politics has a peculiar capacity to devour the soul. As Christian citizens, we must have an obligation to actively support justice, human life, and freedom at home and abroad. So how should all of you utilize political influence as Christians and maintain perspective on our real mission in this world? God will not redeem creation through a political party nor a branch of the government. Christ is monogamous. He has one bride—the church.

Listen carefully, for this is the wisdom God has given to each generation. The best hopes of politics are to be a channel for justice or a positive moral influence on the culture. These are noble pursuits that should not be neglected. But, lasting justice and morality cannot be lobbied for or legislated. It will not come through an act of government. It is a result of the Holy Spirit's work in the lives of those of us who learn that God loves us. So take heed, lest we forget these important labors are always secondary to the gospel, and at times even affect the cause of Christ negatively. Sometimes your perceived political victories are actually spiritual setbacks. True Christianity, the real work of the kingdom, often thrives under fierce attack and opposition. Jesus announced this coming persecution to us, His followers, believing this will lead to our finest hour saying, "The time will come when they will kick you out of the synagogue because some believe God desires them to execute you as an act of faithful service" (16:2).

Jesus never encouraged us to fight for our right to participate in the life of the synagogue. Though we were dejected and hurt by our spiritual exile, God used it for good. The church thrived in exile as non-Jews encountered the story of Christ and spread it passionately, much faster than we as the elect of God could have ever done on our own. Similar dilemmas in your day to come may feel like rejection and failure but may be an open door for God's people to thrive amid adversity.

God will bring all kinds of struggles into your lives to bring glory to Himself and His perfect will. You will be told that all forms of prayer in schools and public places are illegal, but it will actually advance the cause of Christ. You will see a rapid moral decline that actually leads people to an understanding of their sin and their need for God. You will experience Christians having to lead from a place of weakness rather than strength, which in turn will actually bear more spiritual fruit. It should make us stop long enough, when it happens, to reconsider what it is that we are working for—the redemption of the world through Christ, not a place of power.

John 16

Jesus

1 I am telling you all of this so that you may avoid
2 the offenses that are coming. The time will come when they will kick you out of the synagogue because some believe God desires them to
3 execute you as an act of faithful service. They will do this because they don't know the Father,
4 or else they would know Me. I'm telling you all this so that when it comes to pass you will remember what you have heard. It was not important for Me to give you this information in
5 the beginning, when I was with you. But now, I am going to the One who has sent Me, and None of you ask Me, "Where are You going?"
6 I know that hearing news like this is
7 overwhelming and sad. But the truth is that My departure will be a gift that will serve you well, because if I don't leave, the great Helper will not come to your aid. When I leave, I will send Him
8-9 to you. When He arrives, He will uncover the sins of the world, expose unbelief as sin, and

10 allow all to see their sins in the light of righteousness for the first time. This new awareness of righteousness is important because I am going to the Father and will no longer be present

11 with you. The Spirit will also carry My judgment because the one who rules in this world has already been defeated.

12   I have so much more to say, but you
13- cannot absorb it right now. The Spirit of truth
15 will come and guide you in all truth. He will not speak His own words to you, He will speak what He hears, revealing to you the things to come and bringing glory to Me. The Spirit has unlimited access to Me, to all that I possess and know, just as everything the Father has is Mine. That is the reason I am confident He will care for

16 My own and reveal the path to you. For a little while you will not see Me, but after that, a time will come when you will see Me again.

Some of His Disciples 17 What does He mean? "I'll be here, and then I won't be here, because I'll be with the Father."

Other Disciples 18 What is He saying? "A little while?" We don't understand.

[19]Jesus knew they had questions to ask of Him, so He approached them.

The promise of eternity looms over our work in the cosmos as a reminder that we were made for another world. We found great comfort amid our fear in knowing we would be reunited with Christ and joined with the Father. As we labor together in this world, enduring pain, loss, and unfulfilled desires, be encouraged that in eternity all our desires will be fulfilled in the presence of God. Jesus said it this way, "Don't get lost in despair; believe in God and keep on believing in Me. My Father's home is designed to accommodate all of you. If there were not room for everyone, I would have told you that. I am going to make arrangements for your arrival. I will be there to personally greet you and welcome you home, where we will be together. You know where I am going and how to get there" (14:1-4).

Jesus made the point clear to all of us: stay connected with Christ and you will have no reason to fear. Jesus doesn't pronounce that the instant you lay your fears down, you can expect only good things to start happening in your life. In fact, it has nothing to do with present or future circumstances. Ideologies abound that lead you to feed off of your circumstances.

But what if God's favor has nothing to do with our circumstances, promotions, and acclaim, and everything to do with our connection with God and to one another? That is my message to all of you: You will find beauty in unexpected situations. God will show up wrapped in flesh, and then reach His greatest acclaim through a torturous death. If this is all true, then we will find strength and beauty in places we never imagined.

Jesus set the bar of expectations for us very low—expect to be despised and know that many will view killing you as a service to God. This isn't exactly a portrait of the good life. Or is it? Abiding in Jesus Christ is the good life, regardless of the external circumstances.

John 16

Jesus

19 Are you trying to figure out what I mean when

20 I say you will see Me in a little while? I tell you the truth, a time is approaching when you will weep and mourn while the world is celebrating. You will grieve, but that grief will give birth to

21- great joy. In the same way that a woman labors

22 in great pain during childbirth, only to forget the intensity of the pain when she holds her child, when I return, your labored grief will also change

23 into a joy that cannot be stolen.

When all this transpires, you will finally have the answers you have been seeking. I tell

24 you the truth, anything you ask of the Father in My name, He will give to you. Until this moment you have not sought after anything in My name. Ask and you will receive, so that you will be filled

25 with joy.

I have been teaching you all of these truths through stories and metaphors, but the time is coming for Me to speak openly and

26 directly of the Father.

The day is coming when you will make a

27 request in My name, but I will not represent you before the Father. *You will be heard directly by the Father.* The Father loves you because you

28 love Me and know that I come from the Father. I came from the Father into the cosmos but soon I will leave it and return to the Father.

Jesus Teaching

All of us disciples mourned Christ's refusal to take His rightful place as a king and lead a revolution. The other three Gospel writers made it very clear that a spiritual revolution was underway, and Jesus knew that political might, brute force, and earthly governments were not helpful tools in a battle for hearts. Spiritual revolutions are subversive. They are led by defiant acts of love (i.e. healing, foot washing, and martyrdom). Laws do not change hearts, and military force only induces hatred and fear. But a sincere community of faith in which love and hope are demonstrated even in the darkest hours will lead a spiritual revolution. It is time we go forward with open eyes and continue to labor as Christian citizens, but place our hope only in the redemptive work of the gospel.

Disciples	29	We hear You speaking clearly and not in
	30	metaphors. *How could we misunderstand?* We see now that You are aware of everything and You reveal things at the proper time. So we do not need to question You, because we believe You have come from God.
Jesus	31	So you believe now? Be aware that a time is
	32	coming when you will be scattered *like seeds*. You will return to your own way, and I will be left alone. But I will not be alone, because the
	33	Father will be with Me. I have told you these things so that you will be *whole and* at peace. In this world you will be plagued with times of trouble, but you need not fear; I have triumphed over this corrupt world order.

Chapter 5

Connected One to Another

*I*n the days to come, even generations from now, believers will struggle to see how they are connected to God and one another. They will see themselves as autonomous individuals, which is very different than the understanding those of us who walked with Jesus had, which was that of a collective personality. This sense of connectedness to God and one another is important to becoming a true follower of Christ. How can anyone truly be an individual? You belong to a family, a tribe, and your homeland. The very nature of humans is that we grow from within another human, taking on the characteristics of our parents, connecting us back through hundreds of generations. You see, if you are of your mother and father, then you are of your grandparents, great-grand-parents, and so on. You are connected.

Jesus Christ is the Son of our Heavenly Father and through Christ's death and resurrection, we are adopted children into God's forever family. So, now you are in Christ, as am I. So then I am also in you, and you are in me. You and I are connected to God and each other in ways we can't even imagine.

How can you follow Christ if you don't know what it means to be joined with God, to become a living branch in God's vineyard? And remember that grapes do not grow in isolation. Many have romanticized the spiritual path of monasticism—brothers and sisters known for their private journeys into the wilderness to be with God. This word monastic comes from the Greek word *monazein*, meaning, "to be alone." This seems selfish really, and contradicts all that Christ is. Our call is to community, not isolation, to be present with one another, to share, and to raise one another up.

Seasons may come when we are allowed some space that helps us to see the world more clearly and identify God's work in our lives. But we belong to one another. We are to abide in Christ and one another; this is central in Jesus' teachings.

I know these are hard truths. Some of you wonder what difference it makes to believe that we are in Christ and that we are intimately connected with one another. It makes all the difference in the world. You see the world's way is to seek personal advantage, put self first and to live disconnected to everyone else. It is to celebrate the myth of the "self-made man" and to jockey for position over everyone else. But Christ's way is a way of love and connection between God and neighbor. Because we are connected like vines and branches, when we serve one another, we actually serve Christ. And when we serve Christ, we find we have gained great rewards in this life and in the life to come. As Jesus said over and over to us, the way to greatness is service. And no one served us more than Christ.

When Christ was crucified, I suffered His loss immensely. I missed Him, the comfort in His touch and His words. What I discovered in my grief was the strength of Christ's love in communities. My earthly family became the body of Christ to me. They would say comforting things that sounded just like what Jesus would say. They reassured me, encouraged me, and loved me just as He did, proving what Christ taught us from the beginning: we are all connected; not just to the Father and Christ, but also to one another. And, expressing His love, we become a representation of His body here on earth.

John 17

Jesus	**1** *(lifting His face to the heavens)* Father, My time has come. Glorify Your Son, and I will bring You
	2-3 great glory because You have given Me total authority over humanity. *I have come bearing the plentiful gifts of God,* and all that receive Me will experience everlasting life, a new intimate relationship with You, the one true God, and Jesus
	4 Christ (the One You have sent). I have glorified You on the earth and fulfilled the mission You set before Me.
	5 In this moment, Father, fuse Our collective glory and bring Us together as We were before
	6 creation existed. You have entrusted Me with these men who have come out of this corrupt world order. I have told them about Your nature and declared Your name to them, and they have held on to Your words and understood
	7 that these words, like everything else You have
	8 given Me, come from You. It is true, that these men You gave Me have received the words that come from You, and not only understood them
	9 but also believed that You sent Me. I am now making an appeal to You on their behalf. This request is not for the entire world; it is for those whom You have given to Me because they are
	10 Yours. Yours and Mine, Mine and Yours, for all that are Mine are Yours. Through them I have been glorified.
	11 I will no longer be physically present in this world, but they will remain in this world. As I return to be with You, Holy Father, remain with them through Your name, *the name You*

Agony

have given Me. May they be one even as We
12 are one. While I was physically present with
them, I protected them through Your name,
which You have shared with Me. I watched over
them closely and only one was lost, the one
the Scriptures said was the son of destruction.
13 Now I am returning to You. I am speaking this
prayer here in the created cosmos *alongside*
friends and foes so that in hearing it they might
14 be consumed with joy. I have given them Your
word; and the world has despised them because they are not products of the world, in the
same way that I am not a product of the corrupt
15 world order. Do not take them out of this world;
protect them from the evil one.
16   Like Me, they are not products of the cor-
17 rupt world order. Immerse them in the truth, the
18 truth Your voice speaks. In the same way You
19 sent Me into this world, I am sending them. It
is entirely for their benefit that I have set Myself
20 apart, so that they may be set apart by truth. I
am not asking solely for their benefit, this prayer
is also for all the believers who will follow them
21 and hear them speak. Father, may they all be
one as You are in Me and I am in You; may they
be in Us, for by this unity the world will believe
that You sent Me.
22   All the glory You have given to Me, I pass
on to them. May that glory unify them and make
23 them one as We are one; I in them, and You
in Me, that they may be refined so that all will
know that You sent Me, and You love them in
the same way You love Me.

24 Father, I long for the time when those You have given Me can join Me in My place so they may witness My glory, which comes from You. You have loved Me before the foundations of the **25** cosmos were laid. Father, you are just, though this corrupt world order does not know You, I do. These followers know that You have sent **26** Me. I have told them about Your nature, and I will continue to speak of Your name, in order that Your love, which was poured out on Me, will be in them. And I will also be in them.

How is it that we can follow this path and believe these truths of such a Lord? Jesus instructed us to break bread and remember how He allowed His body to be broken for all mankind. Jesus is truly present for all of us in the elements. Touch Him, taste His richness, remember His most glorious hour on the cross. In that moment He embraced all darkness and shame and transformed it into light. As I come to the table with my community, and we feast on His light, life seems more hopeful and complete.

So, come to the Lord's table often. As you take the bread and the wine, you affirm the reality that Christ is among and within you. Then turn and serve your family, Christ's family. Look around and see that Christ is also living within all your brothers and sisters. Then I have no doubt that you will see the cosmos in a different way.

Jesus included us in one of the great secrets that would unfold. He always knew the future. I am sure you wonder what it must have been like to be with Him. There were many surprises and even a few jokes, but what I think you would really like to know about is when Jesus confided to me the identity of His betrayer. That was a dreadful experience. Betrayal by one you love is more painful than the most horrid forms of Roman torture. It cuts deep into your heart and does not allow you the benefit of any kind of defense. But, in Jesus' case, He saw it coming and allowed Himself to be injured. By letting me in on this betrayal before the fact, He shaped my beliefs about what it means to love the way that He loved. Which means that, even when we see betrayal on the horizon, we continue to make ourselves vulnerable. We take on the risk of betrayal by continuing to love. There were many in our community that wanted to love without risk. It's not possible, not in marriage, friendship, or the church—you open yourself to betrayal every time you love.

I did not have any idea when He alluded to Judas that he would be the instigator of such a violent and glorious firestorm. But I knew Jesus was preparing for these days, and in the midst of the terror of His death I found great peace in knowing that Jesus chose this path.

John 18

¹When Jesus finished praying, He began a brief journey with His disciples to the other side of the Kidron Valley, a deep ravine that floods in the winter rains, then farther on to a garden where He gathered His disciples.

²⁻³Judas Iscariot (who had already set his betrayal in motion, and knew that Jesus often met with the disciples in this olive grove) entered the garden with an entourage of Roman soldiers and officials sent by the chief priests and Pharisees. They brandished their weapons under the light of torches and lamps. ⁴Jesus stepped forward. It was clear He was not surprised because He knew all things.

Jesus	Whom are you looking for?
Judas' Entourage	5 Jesus the Nazarene.
Jesus	I am the One.

Judas, the betrayer, stood with the military force. ⁶As Jesus spoke "I am the One," the forces fell back on the ground. ⁷Jesus asked them a second time:

Jesus	Whom are you searching for?
Judas' Entourage	Jesus the Nazarene.
Jesus	8 I have already said that I am the One. If it is Me you are looking for, then let these men go free.

⁹This was spoken to fulfill the prophecy, which says, "None of those entrusted to Me will be lost." ¹⁰Suddenly Peter lunged toward Malchus, one of the high priest's servants and, with his sword, severed the man's right ear.

Jesus	11	*(to Peter)* Put down your sword and return it to the sheath. Am I to turn away from the cup the Father has given Me to drink?

[12]So the Roman commander, soldiers, and Jewish officials arrested Jesus, cuffed His hands and feet, [13]and brought Him to Annas (the father-in-law of Caiaphas the high priest). [14]You may remember that Caiaphas counseled to the Jews that One should die for all people. [15-16]Simon Peter and another disciple followed behind Jesus. When they arrived Peter waited in the doorway while the other disciple was granted access because of his relationship with the high priest. That disciple spoke to the woman at the door, and Peter was allowed inside.

Servant Girl	17	*(to Peter)* You are one of this man's disciples, aren't you?
Peter		I am not.

Chapter 6

Betrayal and Denial

To understand what happened in the garden, you really need to hear how our brother, Matthew, described these events. While the event is the same, Matthew saw things from a different perspective. He was pretty good with details.

Matthew 26

⁴⁷There he was, Judas, leading a crowd of people with swords and clubs; the chief priests and the elders were right there, *ready to arrest Jesus.* ⁴⁸And Judas, the one who intended to betray Him, had said to the elders and the chief priests that he would give them a sign.

Judas | I'll greet Him with a kiss. And you will know that the one I kiss is the one you should arrest.

⁴⁹So at once, he went up to Jesus.

Judas | Greetings, Teacher *(he kisses Him)*.

Jesus | 50 | My friend, why are you here?

And at that, the crowd came, and seized Him. [51]One of the men with Jesus grabbed his sword and swung toward the high priest's slave, slicing off his ear.

Jesus	52	Put your sword back. People who live by the
	53	sword die by the sword. Surely you realize that if I called on My Father He would send twelve
	54	legions of angels to rescue Me? But if I were to do that—well, I would be thwarting the scriptural story, wouldn't I? And we must allow the story of God's kingdom to unfold.

[55]And then Jesus said to the crowds:

| Jesus | | Why did you bring these weapons, these clubs and bats? Did you think I would fight you? That I would try to dodge and escape like a common criminal? You could have arrested Me any day, while I was teaching in the temple—but you didn't. |
| | 56 | This scene has come together just so, so that the prophecies in our sacred Scripture could be fulfilled. |

And at that, all the disciples ran away, and abandoned Him.[57]The crowd that had arrested Jesus took Him to Caiaphas, the high priest. The scribes and elders had gathered at Caiaphas' house, *and were waiting for Jesus to be delivered.* [58]Peter followed Jesus (though at some distance, so as not to be seen). He slipped into Caiaphas' house, and attached himself to a group of servants. And he sat watching, waiting to see how things would unfold.

[59]The high priest and his council of advisors first

produced false evidence against Jesus—false evidence meant to justify some charge, and meant to justify Jesus' execution. [60]But even though there were many men there willing to lie, and fabricate from whole cloth scenes in which Jesus deceived and betrayed, the council couldn't come up with the evidence it wanted. Finally, two men stood up [61]and said:

Two Men   Look, He said 'I can destroy God's temple and rebuild it in three days.' *What more evidence do you need?*

[62]Then, Caiaphas the high priest stood up, and addressed Jesus.

Caiaphas   Aren't You going to respond to these charges? What exactly are these two men accusing You of?

[63]Jesus remained silent. Then the high priest said to Him:

Caiaphas   Under a sacred oath before the living God, tell us plainly: are You the Messiah, the Son of God?

Jesus   64   So you *seem to be* saying, I will say this: beginning now, what you will see is the Son of Man sitting at the right hand of God's power and glory, and coming on heavenly clouds.

[65]The high priest tore his robes and screeched.

Caiaphas   Blasphemy! We don't need any more witnesses—we've all just witnessed this most grievous
        66   blasphemy, right here and now. So, gentlemen:

	What's your verdict?
The Gentlemen	He deserves to die.

[67]Then they spat in His face and hit Him. Some of them smacked Him, slapped Him across the cheeks, [68]and jeered and taunted:

Some of the Men	Well, Messiah. Prophesy for us, if You can—who hit You? *And who is about to hit You next?*

[69]As all this was going on in Caiaphas' chamber, Peter was sitting in the courtyard with some servants. One of the servant girls came up to him.

Servant Girl	You were with Jesus the Galilean, weren't you?

[70]And just as Jesus had predicted, Peter denied it before everyone.

Peter	Not me! I don't know what you're talking about.

[71]He went out to stand by the gate. And as he walked past, another servant girl said:

Another Servant Girl	That man over there—he was here with Jesus the Nazarene!

[72]Again, just as Jesus had predicted, Peter denied it, swearing an oath:

Peter	I don't know Him!

⁷³And Peter went to chat with a few of the servants. A little while later, they said to him:

Other Servants | Look, we know that you must be one of Jesus' followers. You speak like you are from the same area as His followers.

⁷⁴Cursing and swearing, *agitated veins popping up in his forehead, and shoulders growing tense,* Peter said,

Peter | I do not know Him!

As the exclamation point left his mouth, a cock crowed. ⁷⁵And Peter remembered. He remembered that Jesus *had looked at him with something like pity* and said, "This very night, before the cock crows in the morning, you will deny Me three times." And Peter went outside, and sat down on the ground, and wept.

You have to get the picture in your head about what Matthew and I have described to you. Imagine with me that terrible night.

Points of light bobbed and weaved through the trees. A flotilla of lights ascended the Mount of Olives. We didn't have to be omniscient like Jesus to know an ill wind blew through the olive trees of Gethsemane. Judas' kiss, a brief skirmish, and the arrest of Jesus interrupted the quiet of the garden. Bound with ropes and abandoned by us, Jesus was shoved and whipped toward the city by a mob carrying torches and weapons. Had we put up any fight at all, we would have been overwhelmed in seconds by the better-trained and equipped temple guards. Instead, as Jesus predicted, we melted into the blackness. The feeling of loss and betrayal was awful.

Now Caiaphas was high priest at this time. The sacred office he occupied had been corrupted for more than a century by collaboration with Greeks and Romans. Reformers were few, and they had been unable to cleanse the high office from its pollutions. Because of this, many Jews had stopped coming to the temple. How could God's holy habitation on earth be pure if its primary representative was coddling the enemies of Israel? We think that's one of the reasons Jesus released the sacrificial animals and drove out those making profit from the temple. Some said He was cleansing the temple of its ritual defilements. But it seems to me He was announcing its destruction. After what the Romans did in A.D. 70, when they sacked the city and destroyed the temple, what Jesus did and said that day made perfect sense. You see, sometimes prophets speak—sometimes they act out their message.

On this fateful evening Caiaphas had convened a late session of the Sanhedrin at his home to deal with Jesus, the troublemaker from Galilee. The Sanhedrin was the supreme governing council for Jewish affairs around Jerusalem. It managed religious, civil, and political matters in the capital. It was made up of well-heeled Sadducees, scribes, priests, and Pharisees from Judea. Under the Romans, our elders had limited jurisdiction, but that did not always stop them. Caiaphas had instructed his men to bring Jesus to his compound, no matter the hour. What started that night as a preliminary hearing—a legitimate court could only convene during daylight hours—ended in the sentence of death. Some refer to these interrogations as trials, but what transpired over the next hours had nothing to do with justice.

Caiaphas and his friends were looking for something, anything that might justify Jesus' death. He had been a thorn in their sides for years, and they had reached the limit of whatever good will they could muster when Jesus walked into the temple and upset the day's profits earlier that week. Still Jesus had enough sympathizers, and Caiaphas enough enemies on the council, that the high priest couldn't just railroad Him.

False witnesses were brought forward to accuse Jesus. Although many spoke, none of the charges stuck because, according to our laws, the accusation had to be confirmed by at least two witnesses. Some arose and charged Jesus with speaking against the temple. "Finally, two men stood up and said, 'Look, He said "I can destroy God's temple and rebuild it in three days."'" What more evidence do you need?" (Ma 26:61). In fact Jesus had said something like this, but they misrepresented His words and intent. Liars and false witnesses sometimes tell the truth, but never in context.

Finally, Caiaphas turned to Jesus, put Him under oath and asked Him, "Are You the Messiah, the Son of God?" Jesus, who had been stone silent throughout finally gave them what they wanted. He condemned Himself with His words: "So you seem to be saying," said Jesus. "I will say this: Beginning now, what you will see is the Son of Man sitting at the right hand of God's power and glory, and coming on heavenly clouds." Caiaphas heard Jesus' statement, declared it blasphemy, tore his clothes in ritual protest and turned to the representatives of the people: "What is your verdict?" They answered with one voice, "He deserves to die" (Ma 26:64).

It's hard to say what Jesus did to provoke such a response and the charge of blasphemy, a very serious charge indeed. What seemed so obvious to them is still unclear to me. I wasn't there. It came down to me only through reports of those who were. Why was this blasphemy? You see, it is not blasphemy to claim to be the Messiah. Otherwise, how could the real Messiah introduce Himself to us? It must relate then to what Jesus said next. Apparently, Jesus claimed that they will see the Son of Man seated at the right hand of Power, the unspeakable name of God. No one but the high priest was allowed to utter the divine name and then only on Yom Kippur. Perhaps Jesus spoke God's name in this most unholy gathering. I don't know. If Jesus didn't speak the divine name, then it must be what He said next. He claimed to be God's right-hand man and will one day stand as their judge when He comes on the clouds of heaven. It is as if He said: "You may stand in judgment of Me today, but I will stand in judgment of you on the last day." Such arrogance against the Lord's anointed high priest and council could not be tolerated. Jesus stood, condemned of blasphemy, sentenced to die. His own voice uttered the evidence they needed to convict Him. But what were they going to do?

Early the next morning, they decided not only to be rid of Him but also to discredit Him before the crowds. Many were ready to lay down their lives for Him. Crucifixion was the final solution. First, the Roman cross would permanently silence the voice of the Galilean prophet. Second, it would forever put an end to the claim that Jesus was God's Messiah for, according to our laws, everyone who hangs on a tree is under God's curse and the Lord would never allow His anointed to die on a cross. Who in their right mind would follow a crucified Messiah? Now let me get back to the story as I remember it.

John 18

18All the servants and officers gathered around a charcoal fire to keep warm. It was a cold day and Peter made his way into the circle to warm himself.

Annas | 19 | *(to Jesus)* Who are Your disciples and what do You teach?

| Jesus | 20 | I have spoken in public where the world can hear, always teaching in the synagogue and in the temple where the Jewish people gather. I have |
| | 21 | never spoken in secret. So why would you need to interrogate Me? Many have heard Me teach. Why don't you question them? They know what I have taught. |

[22]While Jesus offered His response, an officer standing nearby struck Jesus with his hand.

| Officer | Is that how You speak to the high priest? |

| Jesus | 23 | If I have spoken incorrectly, why don't you point out the untruths that I speak? Why do you hit Me if what I have said is correct? |

[24]Annas sent Jesus to Caiaphas bound as a prisoner. [25]As this was happening, Peter was still warming himself by the fire.

| Servants and Officers | You too are one of His disciples, aren't you? |

| Peter | No, I am not. |

[26]One of the high priest's servants was related to the one assaulted by Peter.

| Servant of the high priest (relative of Malchus) | Didn't I see you in the garden with Him? |

²⁷Peter denied it again, and instantly a rooster crowed.

²⁸Before the sun had risen, Jesus was taken from Caiaphas to the governor's palace. The Jewish leaders would not enter the palace because their presence in a Roman office would defile them and cause them to miss the Passover feast. Pilate, the governor, met them outside.

Pilate	29	What charges do you bring against this man?
Priests and Officials	30	If He weren't a lawbreaker, we wouldn't have brought Him to you.
Pilate	31	Then judge Him yourselves, by your own law.
Jews		Our authority does not allow us to give Him the death penalty.

Initially, Pilate told the Jewish leaders to take Jesus and try Him according to our own laws, but when they hinted at capital charges, Pilate agreed to interrogate Jesus. Rome reserved the right to decide who lived and died in the provinces. They didn't delegate that to the Jewish high council. The charge of blasphemy carried no weight in Roman jurisprudence for it was a matter of our Jewish religious law. Rome had no opinion on such matters. So a new charge must be concocted, a charge that Rome did care about. As Luke puts it, the elders of the people accused Jesus of forbidding us to pay taxes to the emperor and of claiming to be the Messiah, Israel's king (Lk 23:2). Rome did care about taxes, of course, and took a dim view of anyone making royal claims under their noses.

Pilate agreed to hear the charge, not wasting a Roman minute. He took Jesus inside and began asking Him about these charges. The other Gospels—Matthew, Mark, and Luke—provide a kind of public record of what happened that Good Friday. But, I want to take you behind the scenes to the private conversation that took place between Jesus and Pilate.

John 18

³²All these things were a fulfillment of the words Jesus had spoken indicating the way that He would die. ³³So Pilate reentered the governor's palace and called for Jesus to follow him.

Pilate		Are You the King of the Jews?
Jesus	34	Are you asking Me because you believe this is true, or have others said this about Me?
Pilate	35	I'm not a Jew, am I? Your people, including the chief priests, have arrested You and placed You in my custody. What have You done?
Jesus	36	My kingdom is not recognized in this world. If this were My kingdom, My servants would be fighting for My freedom. But My kingdom is not in this physical realm.
Pilate	37	So, You are a king?
Jesus		You say that I am King. For this I have been born, and for this I have come into the cosmos, to demonstrate the power of truth. Everyone who seeks truth hears My voice.

Pilate Presents Jesus

Pilate | 38 | *(to Jesus)* What is truth?

Pilate left Jesus to go and speak to the Jewish people.

Pilate | | *(to the Jews)* I have not found any cause for
| 39 | charges to be brought against this Man. Your
| | custom is that I should release a prisoner to you
| | each year in honor of the Passover celebration;
| | shall I release the King of the Jews to you?

Jews | 40 | No, not this Man! Give us Barabbas!

You should know that Barabbas was a terrorist.

I'd like to have been a fly on the wall when Pilate had that private moment with Jesus. It's clear the governor didn't understand Jesus at all. Pilate was interrogating Jesus like the man he was, an insecure and cruel power broker representing Roman interests in our land. Jesus, though, was doing His typical mustard seed bit, speaking right over the head of the man who later would show Him no mercy. Pilate couldn't handle the truth when he asked, "Are You the King of the Jews?" Jesus was the King of the Jews. And that was the truth. Although Pilate wouldn't recognize it, He was his king, too. But as Jesus knew, the world didn't recognize His kingdom. That's because it was sourced in heaven above, not in Rome. His authority came from God the Father, Creator, Sustainer—not the Roman senate.

Chapter 7

Showing No Fear

*I*t's been my experience that powerful people like Pilate have a hard time understanding Jesus. The rich— not many of them will ever darken the inside of His Kingdom. It's hard. Practically impossible. The rich and powerful by earthly standards often operate with all the wrong categories. For them greatness is often about being served, not serving. It's most likely about coming in first, not struggling to be last. It's almost always about power you can see and fear, not about trusting in the invisible, eternal God.

But there are also a lot of believers, I think, who misunderstand Jesus. When our King said, "My kingdom is not in this physical realm," He didn't mean it was for another time or another place, as if this world didn't matter. No. This world mattered to Jesus and it mattered ultimately. Otherwise, why would He have taken on human flesh and come to be with us? When the Voice became flesh, a piece of this fallen, broken creation became divine. When the Voice rose from the dead, a piece of this fallen, broken creation became eternal. No, my friend, the kingdom of God is about this world. It may be sourced above, in heaven, but its focus, its realm is the cosmos that is our home. Jesus, in fact, taught us to pray everyday, "Bring about Your kingdom. Manifest Your will here on earth, as it is manifested in heaven" (Ma 6:10). If you pray this prayer like I do, every day, then it finally sinks in that the kingdom of God has to do with our lives, here and now. It is the time and place in history when God's will is done on earth as it is in heaven. It's not about going to heaven when we die. It's not about getting us out of here so the world can go to pot. Every day we pray for the King and His kingdom to come; we long for that day. The older I get, the more I ache, the more I long to see His will done on earth.

Back to my story. Jesus stood before the Roman governor the morning of His crucifixion. By sundown His limp body would be lowered from the cross. But He didn't plead for mercy. He remained resolute, even confident when most people would have been terrified.

Pilate, playing both amateur philosopher and professional politician, asked: "What is truth?" How he said it, I'd like to know. What was his tone of voice? What was the look in his eye? Was he mocking Jesus? Was his heart beginning to soften? How Jesus responded is absent from the record. What we know is that Pilate got it wrong. Truth is not a "what"—it's a "who." You remember how Jesus said: "I am the path, the truth, and the energy of life. No one comes to the Father except through Me" (14:6).

You will recall how He promised to pray to the Father that the Spirit of truth would dwell with us and remain with us forever. What Pilate didn't know and what we do know as believers is that he stared Truth in the eye and condemned Him to death.

Now our brother Mark has other details that fill in the story. Listen to how he describes this event.

Mark 15

[1]When morning came, the chief priests met in council with all the Jewish leaders. They bound Jesus and led Him away and turned Him over to the Roman governor, Pilate.

| Pilate | 2 | *(after hearing them)* Are you the King of the Jews? |

| Jesus | | You have said so. |

³The chief priests went on to accuse Jesus of many things, but Jesus simply stood quietly.

| Pilate | 4 | Do You have anything to say? How do You respond to all these charges that have been made against You? |

⁵But Jesus said nothing more, and Pilate was astonished. ⁶Now it was his custom at that feast that Pilate should release one prisoner from custody, whomever the people most desired. ⁷There was one rebel, from those imprisoned for insurrection against the Roman occupation. He had committed murder during an uprising. His name was Barabbas. ⁸A crowd had gathered in front of Pilate's judgment seat to request that Pilate follow his usual custom.

⁹Pilate turned to them.

| Pilate | | Why don't I release to you the King of the Jews? |

¹⁰He knew that the chief priests had delivered Jesus because they were threatened by Him, not because Jesus was a criminal.¹¹But priests moved among the crowd and persuaded them to call for Barabbas instead.

| Pilate | 12 | Then what do you want me to do with the King of the Jews? |

| Crowd | 13 | Crucify Him, *crucify Him!* |

Now crucifixion was a method of capital punishment often used by the Romans, and Pilate had sentenced many people to die on crosses. [14]But now he called to them.

Pilate | Why? What has He done to deserve such a sentence?

Crowd | *(crying out all the louder)* Crucify Him, *crucify Him!*

[15]When Pilate saw that he could not persuade the crowd to change its mind, he released Barabbas to them and had Jesus publicly whipped, which was the normal prelude to crucifixion. Then he had Jesus led away to be crucified. [16]The soldiers took Him into the headquarters of the governor, and the rest of the soldiers in the detachment gathered there, hundreds of them. [17]They put a purple robe on Him, and made a crown of thorns that they forced onto His head, [18]and they began to cry out in mock salute.

Soldiers | Hail to the King of the Jews!

[19]For a long while they beat Him on the head with a reed, and spat upon Him, and knelt down as if to honor Him. [20]When they had finished mocking Him, they stripped off His purple robe and put His own clothes back on Him. Then they took Him away to be executed.

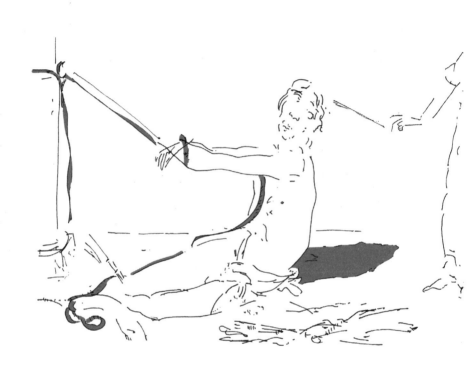

Beaten

Who was this Man, Jesus? He stood quietly yet boldly before the high priest and showed no fear to Pilate. Throughout His life we were continually surprised by Jesus. He was obviously unique. He was unlike anyone we had met before. I remember the time Jesus was awakened from a peaceful rest and rose to face a fierce gale of wind and the stinging spray that came off the Sea of Galilee. Even the seasoned sailors among us were panicking. Jesus rebuked the storm and said, "That's enough! Be still!" Immediately the wind subsided. The rough sea became calm. Jesus turned to us and rebuked us, too, for our lack of faith. In the wake of that storm, we talked among ourselves asking, "Who is this Jesus? How can it be that He has power over even the wind and the waves?" (Mk 4:35-41).

Complicated questions take time to answer. The mystery of Jesus' identity occupied us, and will occupy generations of believers for centuries to come. As we journeyed with Him, it gradually became clearer who this Man was, where He came from, and how His existence would profoundly affect the rest of human history. The question of "Who is this Man?" was not answered overnight. It didn't dawn on us immediately. It was the result of intense thought, debate, searching the Scriptures, and the guidance of the Spirit. Jesus told us that the Heavenly Father would send a Helper, the Holy Spirit, to be our teacher and remind us of all He had said and done (14:26; 15:26-27). Without the Holy Spirit I don't think the mystery would ever have been solved.

As we continued to journey with Jesus, another realization dawned upon us. Matthew tells the story well:

Matthew 16

¹³Jesus then went to Caesarea Philippi , and He asked His disciples:

Jesus | Who do people say the Son of Man is?

Disciples	14	Some say John the Immerser. And some say Elijah. And some say Jeremiah, or one of the other prophets.
Jesus	15	And you? Who do you say that I am?
Simon Peter	16	You are the Christ. You are the Son of the living God.
Jesus	17	Simon, Son of Jonah *("John" in John 21)*, your knowledge is a mark of blessing. For you didn't learn this truth from your friends, or from teachers, or sages you've met on the way. You learned it from My Father in heaven (Ma 16:13-17).

You see, "Christ" is not a name; it is the Greek translation of the Hebrew title "the Messiah." To call Jesus "the Christ" is to confess "Jesus is the Messiah." The term "Messiah" referred to a human being, God's end-time agent destined to bring universal peace and justice to our world. When Simon Peter announced, "You are the Messiah," he spoke for all of us. He was saying more than "Jesus is our rabbi." He was saying, "Here stands God's right-hand man, a man of historic proportion, a man God will use to change the world and history as we know it." But notice—the Messiah that we expected was to be human, not divine. To claim "Jesus is the Messiah" is not to say He is God or one with God. It is to recognize His humanity. Jesus commended Simon for the confession but credited it to the activity of God the Father, not human ingenuity. Jesus accepted the messianic confession from us but warned us not to divulge this prematurely to the crowds. Caution was the word of the day. The stakes were much too high.

Chapter 8

More than a Man

*W*e suspected during His lifetime that Jesus was more than a man, but it took the power and glory of the resurrection to convince us completely that Jesus was divine. When we saw Him, when we touched Him, when the sound of His voice thundered in our souls, we knew we were face-to-face with God's immense glory, the unique Son of God. As we read and reread the Scriptures in light of our experience of Him, we found that Jesus' life and story were the climax of God's covenants with His people.

It was this Lord, this God-Man, that Pilate and the Jewish authorities took to be beaten and humiliated.

John 19

¹Pilate took Jesus and had Him flogged. ²The soldiers twisted thorny branches together as a crown and placed it onto His brow and wrapped Him in a purple cloth. ³They drew near to Him shouting…

Soldiers	*(striking at Jesus)* Bow down, everyone! This is the King of the Jews!
Pilate 4	*(going out to the crowd)* Listen, I stand in front of you with this Man to make myself clear, I find this Man innocent of any crimes.

Crown of Thorns

⁵Then Jesus was paraded out before the people, wearing the crown of thorns and the purple robe.

Pilate		Here is the Man!
Chief Priests and Officers	6	*(shouting)* Crucify, crucify!
Pilate		You take Him and crucify Him; I have declared Him not guilty of any punishable crime!
Jews	7	Our law says that He should die because He claims to be the Son of God.

⁸Pilate was terrified to hear the Jews making their claims for His execution, ⁹so he retired to his court, the Praetorium.

Pilate		*(to Jesus)* Where are You from?

Jesus did not speak.

Pilate	10	How can You ignore me? Are You not aware that I have the authority to either free You or crucify You?
Jesus	11	Any authority you have over Me comes from above, not from your political position. Because of this the one who handed Me to you is guilty of the greater sin.

¹²Pilate listened to Jesus' words and, taking them to heart, he attempted to release Jesus, but the Jews opposed him shouting…

Jews		If you release this Man, you have betrayed Caesar. Anyone who claims to be a king threatens Caesar's throne.

¹³After Pilate heard these accusations, he sent Jesus out and took his seat in the place where he renders judgment. This place was called the Pavement, or Gabbatha in Hebrew. ¹⁴All this occurred at the sixth hour on the day everyone prepares for the Passover.

Pilate		*(to the Jews)* Look, here is your King!
Jews	15	Put Him away, crucify Him!
Pilate		You want me to crucify your King?
Chief Priests		We have no king but Caesar!

¹⁶Pilate handed Him over to his soldiers knowing that He would be crucified. ¹⁷They sent Jesus out carrying His own instrument of execution, the cross, to a hill known as the place of the skull, or Golgotha in Hebrew. ¹⁸In that place they crucified Him along with two others. One was on His right and the other on His left. ¹⁹Pilate ordered that a plaque be placed above Jesus' head. It read, "Jesus of Nazareth, King of the Jews." ²⁰Because the site was near an urban region, it was written in three languages (Greek, Latin, and Hebrew) so that all could understand.

Chief Priests	21	*(to Pilate)* Don't write, 'The King of the Jews.' Write, "He said, 'I am King of the Jews'!"
Pilate	22	I have written what I have written.

²³As Jesus was being crucified, the soldiers tore His outer garments into four pieces, one for each of them. They wanted to do the same with his tunic, but it was seamless, one piece of fabric woven from the top down. ²⁴So they said…

Soldier | *(to other soldiers)* Don't tear it. Let's cast lots, and the winner will take the whole thing.

This happened in keeping with the Scriptures, which said, "They divided My outer garments and cast lots for My clothes." These soldiers did exactly what was foretold in the Scriptures. ²⁵Jesus' mother was standing next to His cross along with her sister, Mary the wife of Clopas, and Mary Magdalene. ²⁶Jesus looked to see His mother, and the disciple He loved, standing nearby.

In Jerusalem Jewish and Roman collaborators arranged with one of the twelve, Judas Iscariot, to arrest Him and bring charges against Him. No one knew what Judas was up to. He died, committed suicide, before anyone had the chance to ask him. But none of these secret plans and intrigue caught Jesus off guard. For some time He had been telling us that He would go to Jerusalem, fall afoul of the authorities, and be crucified. As He predicted, the events unfolded before our eyes on the eve of Passover, spring A.D. 30. They crucified Him publicly on a hill outside the city of Jerusalem. As He hung there, suspended above the world He brought into existence, a few of us stayed close, crowded together for comfort as the divine breath became ever so faint.

Jesus	*John 19*
	(to Mary, His mother) Dear woman, this is your
27	son *(motioning to the beloved disciple)*! This is
	now your mother *(to His disciple)*!

Now you know who "the beloved disciple" is, the last eyewitness to the life, death, and resurrection of Jesus. Mary became family to me, fulfilling the dying wish of Jesus, my Savior. For those of us who gathered at the foot of the cross, family was less about blood kinship than it was about covenant obedience.

Everyone wants to know why I don't talk more about my adopted mother, Mary, in my written Gospel. It's true that Jesus Himself charged me with her care, and I love her as if I were her own son. Caring for her was never a burden, and the reality is that she has always been a simple and private woman. God made her the vessel to bring Christ into the world, and her love for Him was warm and beautiful. Part of me is protective of her, as a son naturally is of his mother. Still, I can see why those who didn't know her would want to learn more about how she lived after Jesus left us, especially those grieving over their own losses. Surely they are looking for answers to how to move forward in their own lives. The truth gives us all great hope. The mother of our Lord served the redemptive purposes of her Son and Savior of us all until her last day on earth. She cared for her family, gave to the poor, and told countless stories about the development of her divine Son. We were always spellbound by her words, and we took pleasure in her kind and encouraging spirit.

Truth is, maybe I shouldn't have, but most of the time I felt completely overwhelmed by the prospect of caring for our Lord's

Crucifixion

mother. Who could take His place? How could I care for her the way that He would have? At some point, I realized that no one could and that Christ was in heaven caring for her and all of us. When I would feel sorry for myself, I just had to think about Jesus. He spent all this time before His death, and through His death showing us how to love and how to serve. He was asking me to do no more in serving Mary than He did in serving us.

It is so hard for us to understand that He would want anything to do with us that we end up not trusting Him to be in charge of our lives. But when we allow Jesus to grow into every corner, every crease of us, then we allow Him to do great things through us. We allow His love to permeate into the world further. We become more compassionate, more patient, more loving.

God became flesh and lived among us, not just to have a transaction with us and ultimately die, but to continue to be with us even when He didn't have to and to send His Spirit to us to be present with us. So, in that, God calls us to something greater, something more significant. It means that we are here as redeeming forces on this earth that the time we are here is about reclaiming the things He has created. We believe that God has created this, the entire cosmos, and that our work here is to say, "This belongs to God," and to help point out the beauty of creation to everyone we know, everyone we meet. And most of all, to live in it ourselves.

John 19

[27]From that moment the disciple treated her like his own mother and welcomed her into his house. [28]Jesus knew now that His work had been accomplished, and the Scriptures were being fulfilled.

| **Jesus** | I am thirsty. |

²⁹A jar of sour wine had been left there; so they took a hyssop branch with a sponge soaked in the vinegar and put it to His mouth. ³⁰When Jesus drank, He spoke…

Jesus | It is finished!

In that moment His head fell, and He gave up the spirit. ³¹The Jews asked Pilate to have their legs broken so the bodies would not remain on the crosses on the Sabbath. It was the day of preparation for the Passover, and that year the Passover fell on the Sabbath. ³²The soldiers came and broke the legs of both the men crucified next to Jesus. ³³When they came up to Jesus' cross, they could see that He was dead, so they did not break His legs. ³⁴Instead, one soldier took his spear and pierced His abdomen, which brought a gush of blood and water.

³⁵This testimony is true; in fact, it is an eyewitness account, and he has reported what he saw so that you also may believe. ³⁶It happened this way to fulfill the Scriptures that "not one of His bones shall be broken" ³⁷and the Scriptures also say, "they will look upon Him whom they pierced."

³⁸After all this, Joseph of Arimathea, a disciple who kept his faith a secret for fear of the Jewish officials, made a request to Pilate for the body of Jesus. Pilate granted his request, and Joseph retrieved the body. ³⁹Nicodemus, who first came to Jesus under the cloak of darkness, brought over one hundred pounds of myrrh and ointments for His burial. ⁴⁰Together, they took Jesus' body and wrapped Him in linens soaked in essential oils and spices, according to Jewish burial customs.

⁴¹Near the place He was crucified, there was a garden with a newly prepared tomb. ⁴²Because it was the day of preparation, they arranged to lay Jesus in this tomb so they could rest on the Sabbath.

Chapter 9

Forsaken but Not Forgotten

I have told you about the other Gospel accounts. I think that it is important for you to hear from the others so that you will have their perspective on what happened. I want you to hear Matthew's words about our Lord's death on the cross before I continue to tell you what I remember about it.

Matthew 27

[23]*Pilate found himself arguing with the crowd.*

Pilate	Why? What crime has this Man committed?
All the People	*(responding with a shout)* Crucify Him!

[24]Pilate saw that he had laid his own trap. He realized that he had given the crowd a choice, and the crowd had chosen, and—unless he wanted a riot on his hands—he now had to bow to their wishes. So he took a pitcher of water, stood before the crowd, and washed his hands.

Pilate	You see to this crucifixion, for this Man's blood will be upon you, not upon me. I wash myself of it.
The Crowd 25	*(responding with vicious glee)* Indeed, let His blood be upon us—upon us and our children!

²⁶So Pilate released Barabbas, and he had Jesus-whom-some-call-the-Messiah flogged, and handed Him over to be crucified.

²⁷The governor's soldiers took Jesus into a great hall, and gathered a great crowd, ²⁸and they stripped Jesus of His clothes and draped Him in a bold scarlet cloak, *the kind that soldiers sometimes wore.* ²⁹They gathered some thorny vines and wove them into a crown and perched that crown upon His head. They stuck a reed in His right hand, and then they knelt before Him, this inside-out, upside-down king. They mocked Him with catcalls:

Soldier	Hail, the King of the Jews!

They did not know that Jesus had already performed the most profound kingly inversion long before, when the King of the universe became a squalling baby in a barn.

³⁰They spat on Him, and whipped Him on the head with His scepter of reeds, ³¹and when they had their fill, they pulled off the bold scarlet cloak, and dressed Him in His own simple clothes, and led Him off to be crucified.

³²As they were walking, they found a man called Simon

of Cyrene, and they forced him to carry the cross. [33]Eventually, they came to a place called Golgotha, which means Place of the Skull. [34]There, they gave Him a drink—wine mixed with bitter herbs. He tasted it but refused to drink it.

[35]And so they had Him crucified.

Let me tell you what the soldiers did as Jesus hung on the cross; what they did with those clothes that once gleamed the whitest white on a transfiguration mountaintop:

[35] They drew lots for His clothes, [36]and they sat on the ground and watched Him hang. [37] They placed a sign over His head. It read, "This is Jesus, King of the Jews." [38]And then they crucified two thieves next to Him, one at His right hand and one at His left hand. *These thieves were King Jesus' retinue.*

[39]Passersby shouted curses and blasphemies at Jesus. They wagged their heads at Him, [40]and hissed.

Passersby	You're going to destroy the temple and then rebuild it in three days? Why don't you start with saving Yourself? Come down from the cross, if You can, if You're God's Son…
Chief Priests, Scribes, Elders	41 *(mocking Him)* He saved others, but He can't save 42 Himself. If He's really the King of Israel, let Him climb down from the cross—then we'll believe 43 Him. He claimed communion with God—well, let God save Him, if He's God's beloved Son.

⁴⁴Even the thieves hanging to His right and left poured insults upon Him. ⁴⁵And then, starting at noon, the entire land became dark. It was dark for three hours. ⁴⁶In the middle of the dark afternoon, Jesus cried out in a loud voice:

Jesus   Eli, Eli, lama sabachthani—My God, My God, why have You forsaken Me?

Bystanders 47   He's calling on Elijah.

⁴⁸One bystander grabbed a sponge, steeped it in vinegar, stuck it on a reed, and gave Jesus the vinegar to drink.

Others 49   We'll see—we'll see if Elijah is going to come and rescue Him.

⁵⁰And then Jesus cried out once more, loudly, and then He breathed His last breath. ⁵¹At that instant, the temple curtain was torn in half, from top to bottom. The earth shook; rocks split in two; ⁵²tombs burst open, and bodies of many sleeping holy women and men were raised up. ⁵³After Jesus' resurrection, they came out of their tombs, and went into the holy city of Jerusalem, and showed themselves to people.
⁵⁴When the Centurion and soldiers who had been charged with guarding Jesus felt the earthquake and saw the rocks splitting and the tombs opening, they were, of course, terrified.

Soldiers   He really was God's Son.

⁵⁵A number of women were present, too, watching from a distance, women who had been devoted to Jesus and followed Him from Galilee. ⁵⁶Mary Magdalene was there, and Mary the

Death of Jesus

mother of James and Joseph, and the mother of the sons of Zebedee.

⁵⁷At evening time, a rich man from Arimathea turned up. His name was Joseph, and he had become a disciple of Jesus. ⁵⁸He went to Pilate and asked to be given Jesus' body; and Pilate assented, and ordered his servants to turn Jesus' body over to Joseph. ⁵⁹So Joseph took the body, wrapped Jesus in a clean sheath of white linen, ⁶⁰and he laid Jesus in his own new tomb, which he had carved from a rock. Then he rolled a great stone in front of the tomb's opening, and he went away. ⁶¹Mary Magdalene was there, and so was the other Mary. They sat across from the tomb, watching, remembering.

⁶²The next day, which is the day after the Preparation Day, the chief priests and the Pharisees went together to Pilate. ⁶³They reminded him that when Jesus was alive, He had claimed that He would be raised from the dead after three days.

| **Chief Priests and Pharisees** | 64 | So please order someone to secure the tomb for at least three days. Otherwise, His disciples might sneak in and steal His body away, and then claim that He has been raised from the dead—and if that happens—well, we would have been better off just leaving Him alive. |
| **Pilate** | 65 | You have a guard. Go on and secure the grave. |

⁶⁶So they went to the tomb, sealed the stone in its mouth, and put a soldier on guard to keep watch.

As the lifeless body of Jesus was laid into the virgin tomb, those of us who witnessed the spectacle retreated into the city that had claimed the lives of so many prophets. All of us were crushed that our teacher and friend had died such a horrible death. Our hopes were dashed against the rocks of Golgotha. In the first hours of our grief, we huddled together in secret in the city, hoping to avoid our own arrests and executions. We mourned. We grieved. We remembered. Three days later some of us ventured outside the city and returned to the place where He was buried. Miraculously, the stone was rolled back and the rock-hewn tomb empty. Had someone taken His body? Were His enemies laying a trap for us? Or perhaps could it be . . . that the last days were here?

Now I want you to know what I remember of that glorious day.

John 20

¹Before the sun had risen on Sunday morning, Mary Magdalene made a trip to the tomb where Christ's body was laid to rest. In the darkness she discovered the covering had been rolled away. ²She darted out of the garden to find Simon Peter and the dearly loved disciple to deliver this startling news.

Mary Magdalene | They have taken the body of our Lord, and we cannot find Him!

³*Together* they all departed for the tomb to see for themselves. ⁴They began to run and Peter could not keep up. The beloved disciple arrived first ⁵but did not go in. There was no corpse in the tomb, only the linens and cloths He was wrapped in. ⁶When Simon Peter finally arrived, he went into the tomb and observed the same: ⁷The cloth that covered His face appeared to have been folded carefully and placed, not with the linen

cloths, but to the side. [8]After Peter pointed this out, the other disciple (who had arrived long before Peter) also entered the tomb and, based on what he saw, faith began to well up inside him! [9]Before this moment, none of them understood what it meant when the Scriptures said, "He must be raised from the dead." [10]Then they all went to their homes.

[11]Mary, however, stood outside the tomb sobbing, crying, and kneeling at the entrance of the tomb. [12]As she cried, two angels appeared before her sitting where Jesus' head and feet had been laid.

Two Angels	13	Dear woman, why are you weeping?
Mary Magdalene		They have taken away my Lord, and I cannot find Him.

[14]After uttering these words she turned around to see Jesus standing before her, but she did not recognize Him.

Jesus	15	Dear woman, why are you sobbing? Who is it you are looking for?

She still had no idea who it was before her. Thinking He was the gardener, she muttered:

Mary Magdalene		Sir, if you are the one who carried Him away, then tell me where He is and I will retrieve Him.
Jesus	16	Mary!
Mary Magdalene		*(she turns to Jesus and tries to hug Him; speaking in Hebrew)* Rabboni, my Teacher!

Jesus Appears to Mary

Jesus | 17 | Mary, you cannot hold Me. I must rise above this world to be with My Father, who is also your Father, My God who is also your God. Go tell this to all My brothers.

¹⁸Mary Magdalene obeyed and went directly to His disciples.

Mary Magdalene | *(announcing to the disciples)* I have seen the Lord and this is what He said to me…

The hope of resurrection had often been a topic on the lips of Jesus. As He painted a picture of this glorious age in prophetic verse, we felt strangely warmed by the prospect. Now it was taking shape in our time. Confusion gave way to conviction as Jesus appeared to us alive over the next few Sundays. One by one He convinced us that God had raised Him from the dead, and that the general resurrection had begun just as the prophet Daniel had said, "And many of those who sleep in the dust of the earth will wake up—some to abundant life in the new world God is creating, and others to utter disgrace and endless shame. Those who embrace wisdom will shine like the sky on a bright summer's day, and those who lead the journey to a just world will twinkle like the stars above, forever and ever" (Da 12:2-3).

Chapter 10

The Mantle of Forgiveness

*I*n His final days with us, Jesus commissioned those who remained to stop at nothing with the message His Spirit was writing on our hearts. He told us to carry this good news to the ends of the earth so that all the nations could hear and receive salvation. But the same forces that threatened Jesus now stood in the way of us who prayed, baptized, and performed miracles in His name. Despite this, bold confidence eclipsed every whimper of fear that paralyzed us at first. Even with continual threats of imprisonment and violence hanging over us, we stepped into the light of day with His message.

You must hear how Matthew recorded these strange events. It is only by looking at what each of us has recorded that you can get the full impact of the story.

Matthew 28

¹After the Sabbath, as the light of the next day crept over Palestine, Mary Magdalene and the other Mary came to the tomb to keep vigil. ²Earlier, there had been an earthquake. An angel of the Lord had come down from heaven and had gone to the grave. He rolled away the stone and sat down on top of it. ³He veritably glowed. He was vibrating with light, His clothes were

light, white like transfiguration, like new dogwood. [4]The soldiers guarding the tomb were terrified. They froze like stone.

[5]The angel spoke to the women, to Mary Magdalene and the other Mary:

Angel | [6] | Don't be afraid. I know you are here keeping watch for Jesus who was crucified. But Jesus is not here. He was raised, just as He said He would be. Come over to the grave, and see for yourself. And then, go straight to His disciples, and tell them that He's been raised from the dead and that He has gone on to Galilee. You'll find Him there. Listen carefully to what I am telling you.

with [7] marking "yourself. And then..."

[8]The women were both terrified and thrilled, and they left the tomb, quickly, left the tomb and went to find the disciples and give them this outstandingly good news. [9]But while they were on their way, they saw Jesus Himself.

Jesus | Peace.

The women fell down before Him, kissing His feet and worshiping Him.

Jesus | [10] | Don't be afraid. Go, and tell My brothers to go to Galilee. Tell them I will meet them there.

[11]As the women were making their way to the disciples, some of the soldiers who had been standing guard by Jesus' tomb recovered themselves and went to the city and told the chief priests everything that had happened—*the earthquake just after dawn, the angel, the angel's commission to the Marys.*

[12]The chief priests gathered together all the elders, an emergency conference of sorts. They needed a plan. They decided the simplest course was bribery: bribe the guards, pay them off [13]and order them to say that the disciples had come in the middle of the night and had stolen Jesus' corpse. [14]They promised the soldiers they'd run interference with the governor, so that the soldiers wouldn't be punished for falling asleep when they were supposed to be keeping watch. [15]The guards took the bribe, and spread the story around town—and indeed, you can still find people today who will tell you that Jesus did not really rise from the dead, that it was a trick, some sort of sleight of hand.

[16]The eleven disciples, having spoken to the Marys, headed to Galilee, to the mountain where they were to meet Jesus. [17]When the disciples saw Jesus there, many of them fell down and worshiped, like Mary and the other Mary had done. But a few hung back. They were not sure *(And who can blame them?)*. *They did not know, not for sure, what to do or how to be.* [18]Jesus came forward and addressed His beloved disciples. This is what He said:

Jesus	I am here speaking with all the authority of God, who has commanded Me to give you this commission:
19	Go out and make disciples in all the nations. Baptize them in the name of the triune God:
20	Father, Son, and Holy Spirit. Then disciple them. Form them in the practices and postures that I have taught you, and show them how to follow the commands I have laid down for you. And I will be with you, day after day, to the end of the ages. And so now: Begin.

Keep these words from Matthew in mind as I continue my account of the events after Jesus was raised from the dead.

John 20

[19]On that same evening (Resurrection Sunday), the followers gathered together behind locked doors in fear that some of the Jewish leaders in Jerusalem were still searching for them. Out of nowhere, Jesus appeared in the center of the room.

Jesus | May each one of you be at peace.

[20]As He was speaking, He revealed the wounds in His hands and side. The disciples began to celebrate as it sunk in that they were really seeing the Lord.

Jesus | 21 | I give you the gift of peace. In the same way the Father sent Me, I am now sending you.

[22]Now He drew close enough to each of them that *they could feel His breath.* He breathed on them:

Jesus | 23 | Welcome the Holy Spirit of the living God. You now have the mantle of God's forgiveness. As you go, you are able to share the life-giving power to forgive sins, or withhold forgiveness.

[24]All of the eleven were present with the exception of Thomas. [25]He heard the accounts of each brother's interaction with the Lord.

The Other Disciples	We have seen the Lord!
Thomas	Until I see His hands, feel the wounds of the nails, and put my hand to His side, I won't believe what you are saying.

[26]Eight days later, they gathered again behind locked doors and Jesus reappeared. This time Thomas was with them.

Jesus	May each one of you be at peace.

[27]He drew close to Thomas and said:

Jesus		Reach out and touch Me. See the punctures in My hands, reach out your hand and put it to My side, leave behind your faithlessness and believe.
Thomas	28	*(filled with emotion)* You are the one true God, and Lord of my life.
Jesus	29	Thomas, you have faith because you have seen Me. Blessed are all those who never see Me and yet they still believe.

[30]Jesus performed many other wondrous signs that are not written in this book. [31]The accounts are recorded so that you, too, might believe that Jesus Christ is the Son of God, because believing grants you the life He came to share.

To be sure, the Spirit was strong with our first church in Jerusalem. It grew mightily. At first, the Jesus movement, as I've heard some call it, stayed within the bounds of our maternal faith. We were Jewish followers of the Jewish Jesus and most, if not all, continued to live as Jews: observing the Sabbath, worshiping in the synagogues and temple, circumcising our male children on the eighth day, eating kosher diets, and maintaining a strict separation between us Jews and the non-Jews. We didn't understand completely what the Spirit of truth was about to do. Jesus had come, we thought, not to found a new religion but to reform and restore an old religion that had lost its way. But the new wine of the Kingdom could not be contained in the old wineskins of human traditions. New wineskins had to be created in order to channel and flex with the Spirit's power. For some of us the newness came as welcome as a summer shower. For others, particularly those outside our circle, the movement threatened their status and power. The clash between the old and new was inevitable.

Jesus Appears to the Disciples

Chapter 11

Caught Any Fish?

We didn't know what to do with ourselves. What we all knew was fishing. So—we went fishing. We wanted to feel comfortable again. What we found was, our old ways of life were not comforting anymore. What we were doing wasn't working. Jesus never taught us how to turn two fish into a mound of food that could feed thousands, and Judas had all our money. So, if we wanted to eat, then we had to go catch some fish. Grief has a way of stripping you down to basic survival skills. We were still trying to wrap our brains around what happened and why. And it's only natural when you are suffering great loss to try to comfort yourself by doing what you know. We couldn't even catch our own bait, and Peter gets real grumpy when he is hungry.

We were a band of fishermen who were lost and lonely. But just when we thought things couldn't become stranger, Jesus showed up. He told us to fish on the other side of the boat. We did, and we were suddenly overwhelmed with fish. The nets were bulging.

It's just like Jesus to show up in such a simple way and put plainly before our eyes what He wants to teach us. He could have just told us our lives were empty without Him and His work (we already knew that anyway). Instead, what He showed us here, is that not only would our lives be as empty as our nets, but that our old ways of comforting ourselves, our old habits were not going to work for us anymore. He had impacted our lives in a way that changed us forever. We couldn't go back. And He knew we didn't know how to go forward.

John 21

¹There was one other time when Jesus appeared to the disciples—this time by the Sea of Tiberias. This is how it happened: ²Simon Peter, Thomas (called Didymus), Nathanael (the Galilean from Cana), the sons of Zebedee, and two other disciples were together:

Simon Peter	3	*(to disciples)* I am going fishing.
Disciples		Then we will come with you.

They went out in the boat and caught nothing through the night. ⁴As day was breaking, Jesus was standing on the beach, but they did not know it was Jesus.

Jesus	5	My sons, you haven't caught any fish, have you?
Disciples		No.
Jesus	6	Throw your net on the starboard side of the boat and your nets will find the fish.

They did what He said, and suddenly they could not lift their net because of the massive weight of the fish that filled it. ⁷The disciple loved by Jesus turned to Peter and said:

Beloved Disciple | It is the Lord.

Immediately, when Simon Peter heard these words, he threw on his shirt (which he would take off while he was working) and dove into the sea. [8]The rest of the disciples followed him, bringing in the boat and dragging in their net full of fish. They were close to the shore, fishing only about one hundred yards out. [9]When they arrived on shore, they saw a charcoal fire laid with fish on the grill. He had bread, too.

Jesus | 10 *(to disciples)* Bring some of the fish you just caught.

[11]Simon Peter went back to the boat to unload the fish from the net. He pulled 153 large fish from the net. Despite the number of the fish, the net held without a tear.

Some people have wondered how and why I remembered how many fish we caught that day. It's been a long time, but let me tell you why.

Whenever we went fishing, it was our custom to take some fish home to our families and take the rest to the market. Fish don't keep long and you have to cook them that day. As we were counting the fish to divide them up among the workers, we noticed something. I say "we," but I really mean one of the other brothers. Fishermen are practical people by in large and not given to mysticism. But not everybody there made his living with the nets. One of the others, however, had studied gematria. That is a kind of spiritual reflection, a mystical wisdom based on the numbers associated with the letters in our alphabet. In gematria numbers are symbols of great spiritual truths. Some believe that God uses these numbers as guides to deep mysteries and meaning. Anyway, as we divided up the catch, we noticed there were 153 fish. We learned that day from one of the brothers that 153 is the number in gematria for the phrase "the sons of God." When I heard that, standing among the fish and the nets beside the boat, it suddenly dawned on me what we had become. By following Jesus and believing in Him, we had changed. We had become "the sons of God." Now it was our job to fish for people so they too can become "the sons of God." Thomas, always the doubter, waved it off, mumbling, "it's just a coincidence." Others stooped down and wrote in the sand trying to find some other hidden message. But me? I just think there may be something to it.

After spending time with Jesus, I realize there are no coincidences. He revealed to me a world where God is intimately involved, the main actor in the drama of history. It was no accident that we caught the fish. It was no accident the nets didn't break. These fish, all 153, were a sign from God, representing the community of believers, men and women transformed by faith. Some of us sat down and didn't say a word as we pondered all of this. Others busied themselves in work, their hands moving quickly to stack the catch in baskets and untangle the nets. Each in his own way thought, wondered, and prayed. I have to admit, the prospect of it all still makes me smile.

That's how I always begin and end my stories of Jesus. I remind my little children that through faith He gives us the authority to become the sons of God. Brother Paul says it's all grace. He's right. We are what we are because of His wonderful work in us. The challenge we face everyday is to become what we are—His loving, devoted children. To do that, we have to strip away every vestige of our old life. Like worn out clothes, we find our former lives aren't able to contain the beauty of this new creation. Before we can put on the new life and take up our new calling, we have to set aside every ugly and broken aspect of our lives. Repentance, Jesus told us, is not just about what you put off. It's about what you put on. In the human spirit, there is no vacuum. Something will always occupy you and fill your life. It is either life from above or death from below. If the resurrection of Jesus taught us anything, it's that He is the resurrection and the life. I'm not talking about life after death. What I mean is that through Jesus we can have abundant life, a full and meaningful life, here and now.

But more happened that day on the beach. Jesus had made breakfast.

Jesus | 12   Come and join Me for breakfast.

Not one of the disciples dared to ask, "Who are You?" They knew it was the Lord. [13]Jesus took the bread and gave it to each of them, and then He did the same with the fish. [14]This was the third time the disciples had seen Jesus since His death and resurrection. [15]They finished eating breakfast.

Jesus	Simon, son of John, do you love Me more than these other things?
Simon Peter	Yes, Lord. You know that I love You.
Jesus	Take care of My lambs.

[16]Jesus asked him a second time…

Jesus Appears to Peter

Jesus		Simon, son of John, do you love Me?
Simon Peter		Yes, Lord. You *must surely* know that I love You.
Jesus		Shepherd My sheep.
Jesus	17	*(for the third time!)* Simon, son of John, do you love Me?

Peter was hurt because He asked him the same question a third time, "Do you love Me?"

Simon Peter		Lord, You know everything! You know that I love You.
Jesus	18	Look after My sheep. I tell you the truth, when you were younger you would pick up and go wherever you pleased; but when you grow old, someone else will help you and take you places you do not want to go.

[19]Jesus said all this as an indicator of the nature of Peter's death, which would glorify God. After this conversation Jesus said...

Jesus		Follow Me!

When Jesus took Simon Peter off to the side to speak to him, the rest of us knew what was about to happen. Simon had told us how he denied Jesus three times. He felt awful about it. He felt small. He felt he had betrayed Jesus. We all sensed that Jesus knew about this, too. Up to that point neither Simon Peter nor Jesus had brought it up. But eventually someone had to deal with it. They sat far enough away that we couldn't hear what was said. We tried to look busy, like we didn't notice. But we did. We eventually found ourselves looking over that way, crowded on the beach, straining to overhear something, anything of the conversation. Simon told us later how it went, what Jesus said. I think that conversation on the beach that day affected him profoundly. From then on Simon was one of the most humble men I knew.

What got everyone's attention was that Jesus called him "Simon." He hadn't done that in years. From the time that Jesus gave him the nickname "Peter" ("the Rock"), He had always referred to him by that name. But "Peter" hadn't felt like "the Rock" ever since the night Judas betrayed us. As Peter warmed himself by the fire in the high priest's court, he betrayed Jesus, too, by denying he even knew Jesus. For days, he felt miserable, a complete traitor. Jesus knew that so when it came time to give him "the talk," He called him "Simon."

Chapter *12*

Jesus Is Lord

*W*hat Jesus did next was nothing short of brilliant. Three times He asked Simon whether he loved Him. Each time Simon said something like, "Yes, Lord. You know that I love You." Simon was perturbed that Jesus asked him the same question three times. But later he figured it out, with my help, I might add. Three times Simon denied Him. Now Jesus gave him three chances to repent, confess his love, and be restored. Face-to-face with His Lord he declared his love, and as he did, he felt the burden of his betrayal lift. He began to feel more like the rock he was. Jesus forgave him and then commissioned him to take care of His people. We all took notice. Jesus didn't just forgive him and then offer him some menial task. Our Master put Peter, the Rock, in charge. Since then, Peter's been prominent among us—some have even said a bit too prominent. But it's what Jesus wanted.

We all learned a lesson that day. No matter what we have done, no matter the weight of our burden and sin, our Master wants to forgive us and restore us to be the people He made us and called us to be. Something happens when we confess our love for Jesus. We are transformed. Our burdens lift. And we see clearly, more clearly than before, what He wants us to be and do. Repentance means more than making a list of all our wrongs. We know already what they are. They weigh us down everyday. What is as important as confessing our faults is the positive confession of our love for God, hearing His voice and doing what He asks.

John 21

²⁰Peter turned around to see the disciple loved by Jesus following the two of them; the one who leaned back on Jesus' side during their supper and asked, "Lord, who is going to betray You?"

Peter | 21 Lord, and what will happen to this man?

Jesus | 22 If I choose for him to remain till I return, what difference will this make to you? You follow Me!

²³It is from this exchange with Jesus that some thought this disciple would not die. But Jesus never said that. He said, "If I choose for him to remain till I return, what difference will this make to you?" ²⁴That very same disciple is the one offering this truthful account written just for you. ²⁵There are so many other things that Jesus said and did, and if these accounts were also written down the books could not be contained in the entire cosmos.

Initially all of us stayed in Jerusalem, basking in the glow of the Spirit and the power of His presence. It took a wave of persecution to dislodge us from David's capital to take the message to Judea, Samaria, and the ends of the earth. We really didn't know what to expect. The suffering we faced was a surprise, but we should have anticipated it. Jesus suffered, why would it be any different for us? What He is showing us is that the fruits of our labor will be

Ascension

108   the last eyewitness: the final week

so much sweeter when they are rooted in His mission. We could fish all day on our own, and maybe get enough fish to feed ourselves for the rest of our days. Or we can fish with Jesus and catch enough to feed the world.

But, then He turns it around on us and says, "Do you love Me more than these?" In other words, how can you still love your old life after all I have done? Do you find fulfillment in what you used to? I have changed you, and from here on out your life is going to be about so much more than fishing—or working, or just surviving. Your old way of life, your old way of comforting is not going to work anymore. I am going to comfort you, and it is going to be in ways you can't even imagine.

He lays out this choice like He did on the beach when He laid fish on the grill…you can stay here if you want, and drown in grief, spend the rest of your days trying to feed your own hunger. Or you can follow Me, serve My people, and feast on My endless love. What He is saying is that our lives are about more than just feeding ourselves; it's about feeding the world. We were all transformed on that day, not just Peter. We found ways to serve God faithfully, and many of my brothers suffered torture, imprisonment, and death for their faithfulness to Christ and His sheep.

As we left our moorings in Jerusalem, we came face-to-face with peoples of different colors, languages, religions, and cultures. As the people of the Messiah, we were now about to encounter one of our greatest challenges. How should these uncircumcised pagans be included in the congregation of God's Messiah? Should they be required to live like we Jews or could they enter by faith in Christ alone? Led by Peter, James (the Lord's brother), and Paul, we set a course. We. We decided, after several rough years of rancor and debate, that the only condition for entering the church and receiving salvation was faith in Christ alone. In other words, Gentiles didn't have to live like Jews in order to be saved. Some cite this decision as the fracture which forever separated the people of the first and second covenants. Perhaps. Perhaps not. It was not long until we were banished from the synagogues where we had worshiped all our lives. Apparently, the message of a crucified Messiah created too much dissonance for orthodox ears.

Despite all the strife we experienced in those days, I'm still not entirely certain why so many non-believing Jews considered our movement so dangerous. Some, I think, were very upset at the prospect of reclining at the table with Gentiles for supper, because it would make them unclean under the law. They couldn't imagine that kind of table fellowship. To us it was plain what God wanted to happen. The Lord was creating a new kind of world where those distinctions didn't ultimately matter. Those barriers were supposed to come down. Others, I'm sure, were worried that our claim that Jesus was the Messiah would bring down the wrath of Rome. We all sort of expected it would. I suppose the claim that "Jesus is Lord" didn't sit well with Caesar. But we didn't care. We knew it was true. But I think the real reason we were cast out of the synagogues was our religious devotion to Jesus, not just as Rabbi, Prophet, and Messiah, but as Lord.

We composed hymns in His honor, offered Him prayers, and called upon Him in our worship. Outsiders, I suspect, thought we had abandoned our conviction that God is One. But we hadn't. We were still fully convinced of that. What we knew, however, as a result of our time with Jesus, was that God had become flesh. Somehow this Man, Jesus, manifested God's life in our midst. Now that's a pretty big idea for a fisherman. I'll let people smarter than I am figure that one out. But I'll go to my grave bearing witness that it is true.

Regardless of why it happened, a shift was underway that resulted eventually in two of the world's great religions: Judaism and Christianity. Like Rebekah's children, Jacob and Esau, Judaism and Christianity are twins from the same womb. They have the same mother, the same Father, and the same spiritual DNA. Yet they are two separate faiths with important differences, journeys, and destinies.

In my day it had become clear that the followers of Jesus were no longer welcome in the synagogues and temple. This situation resulted after decades of bitter envy and strife. Family conflict is always the most heartrending and painful. The careful reader of my Gospel will see the friction between Jesus and "the Jews." You see it on nearly every page. These early episodes of controversy that swirled around Jesus initially have been called "the parting of the ways," the eventual separation of the Jesus movement from its spiritual kin. Christian readers must be careful not to read their later broken history with Jewish people back into these texts. As the last eyewitness, I see the fruit of unresolved family conflicts that began initially in Jesus' own ministry.

Like I said—at the end, I could pull out stories about Jesus, miracles, forgiveness and everlasting life until the end of time (and I would, but contrary to rumor and popular opinion, I didn't live forever). I am old, tired. I have well outlived my brothers who one after another were sacrificed for this holy mission. It is all just as Christ predicted. And, I plan on telling these stories until the very end with an undying hope that these stories will not die with me. Besides, they are not mine to keep. I hope you will come to know my story, well enough in fact that you could tell it to people.

This week changed me forever. I no longer fear death—neither should you. I have found that loving others is the greatest gift in life—I pray you have learned this too.

I quit waiting for others to serve me and began to give of myself—stop hoarding and consuming and lose yourself in the act of service.

I quit worrying. Because I found out that your worst fears can come to fruition (i.e. losing Christ in a brutal execution) and God can use what seems to be a nightmare to rescue humanity from their own sin and torture.

So, live life fully in devotion to Christ and remember the advice I gave to people like you thousands of times. You need not be confused about what you are to do in life. It has all been made crystal clear—Love one another.

In the end, my health will fail and I too will return home. I have lived a full and exciting life serving God and loving His children. I pray that in sharing this story with you that I have passed on a piece of what Christ gave to me. And, in this way—as it was with Jesus—I hope you do the same. This is the greatest story, and it's all true—you have the promise of the Last Eyewitness.

Epilogue

More than any other Gospel, the Gospel of John provided the early church with the raw materials it needed to recognize and express the deity of Christ and, ultimately, the doctrine of the Trinity. The prologue (1:1-18) describes Jesus as the Logos, the Word of God, preexistent with God from the beginning, the Creator of all that is, God in human flesh. Yet this Word is not merely one mode of God's existence or one phase of God's history. This Logos is distinct from the Father yet one with Him, a mystery indeed of existence and the Ground of Being. This Logos makes visible the invisible God and reveals Him to a dark, lifeless world. As John recalls the words of the incarnate Word, he relates how Jesus and the Father move and work as one.

"The truth is that the Son does nothing on His own; all these actions are led by the Father. The Son watches the Father closely and then mimics the work of the Father" (5:19).

"The Father can give life to those who are dead; in the same way the Son can give the gift of life to those He chooses" (5:21).

"The Father radiates with life and He also animates the Son of God with the same life-giving *beauty and* power to exercise judgment over all of creation" (5:26-27).

"I have not ever, and will not in the future, act on My own. I listen to the directions of the One who sent Me, and act on these divine instructions. For this reason, My judgment is always fair and never self-serving" (5:30).

According to John, the Father and the Son share an intimacy born in a common will and unity of action. In all they do to effect the salvation of humanity, the Son takes His cue from the Father. In every way the Son depends upon, and is ultimately subordinate to the Father. But there is more to this relationship than meets the eye. Upon the lips of Jesus, the "I am" statements echo God's covenant name revealed to Moses at the burning bush (Ex 3:13-15).

"I am the bread that gives life. If you come to My table and eat, you will never go hungry. Believe in Me, you will never go thirsty" (6:35).

"I am the light that shines through the cosmos; if you walk with Me you will thrive in the nourishing light that gives life and will not know darkness" (8:12).

"I am the resurrection and the source of all life; those who believe in Me will live even in death. Everyone who lives and believes in Me will never truly die" (11:25-26).

"I am the path, the truth, and the energy of life. No one comes to the Father except through Me. If you know Me, you know the Father. Rest assured now, you know Him and have seen Him" (14:6-7).

These provocative claims made by Jesus caused His followers to see Him in a whole new light. They bestowed upon Him the name above every name, God's covenant name, and bowed before Him in worship. This kind of devotion to Christ didn't detract in any way from their devotion to God. Indeed to worship Jesus and call Him "Lord" is to glorify God and do His will (Ph 2:9-11). But the opponents of Jesus found these sayings so offensive that they accused Him of blasphemy, the charge that ultimately nailed Him to the cross.

On the last night of His earthly life, the Voice spoke again of His relationship to the Heavenly Father.

(to Philip) "I have lived with you all this time and you still don't know who I am? If you have seen Me, you have seen the Father. How can you keep asking to see the Father?" (14:9).

"Father, may they all be one as You are in Me and I am in You; may they be in Us, for by this unity the world will believe that You sent Me" (17:21).

"All the glory You have given to Me, I pass on to them. May that glory unify them and make them one as We are one;" (17:22).

With these words the last eyewitness put the finishing touches on his portrait of Jesus. For him the unity of the Son with the Father was more than an ideal to strive for; it was the reality of God's essential nature. To see Jesus is to see the Father because they are indeed one.

One of the earliest confessions by the followers of Jesus was "Jesus is our Rabbi, our Teacher." As they walked with Jesus, heard His parables, listened to Him explain Scripture, and heard His vision of the coming kingdom of God, they decided to become His pupils. Some, like John, the last eyewitness, became part of an inner circle that was with Jesus at all the important events in His ministry. Others were part of "the twelve," a group of men Jesus chose intentionally to embody and represent the new people of God for the last days. An even larger group of men and women made up the rest of His "disciples," the school of this great Rabbi.

By calling Jesus their Rabbi, they agreed to watch His life, imitate Him, and follow His teachings.

Another important, Christological moment came after Jesus' death and resurrection. As the risen Jesus appeared to His disciples on a series of Sundays, they came to believe the unbelievable news that Jesus was alive from the dead. One of the twelve, Thomas—the one we call "doubting Thomas"—was not present the first time Jesus appeared to them. He found the claim that Jesus conquered death incredible and said he wouldn't believe until he witnessed it with his own eyes. On the next Sunday the risen Jesus appeared again and turned directly to Thomas and said: "Reach out and touch Me. See the punctures in My hands, reach out your hand and put it to My side, leave behind your faithlessness and believe" (20:27).

Thomas, dumbfounded, uttered the memorable statement: "You are the one true God, and Lord of my life" (20:28).

Although the first believers were Jews and monotheists, their understanding of God was radically altered by their encounter with Jesus and the Holy Spirit. As the Revealer, Jesus provided them with a new vision and understanding of God. Therefore, they discovered that God's oneness must be understood in light of this new revelation. The monotheism that Jews confessed in the Shema (De 6:4-6) was not a strict, mathematical oneness; it was a unity expressed through the plurality of God's manifestations through history.

In our time, as more than a billion Christians gather for worship, we sing praises to the blessed Trinity and recite creeds that profess faith in God the Father, God the Son, and God the Holy Spirit. Every year millions are baptized into the name of the Father, Son, and Holy Spirit. The doctrine of the Trinity is the church's final answer to the question raised by the disciples in the boat that day: "Who is this Man?" The story of how we arrived at this Trinitarian mystery is a fascinating and complicated one.

Entire books have been written on the subject. In nearly every generation some scholar takes a new angle on this puzzling and important theological question. Our journey through the last portion of the Gospel of John has given us a glimpse at some of the key moments in that story.

Later generations of Christians continued to reflect on the stories and traditions handed down to them from the apostles and prophets. They mined the sayings and deeds of Jesus found in the Fourth Gospel to sculpt a Christology that included Jesus within the divine identity and yet kept Him a separate and distinct person. As competing visions of the church and its Lord arose, bishops and other leaders met in places like Nicea, Ephesus, Constantinople, and Chalcedon to hash out the language of what the true faith really held. In all those debates there were winners and losers. Still Christians today of every stripe—Catholic, Eastern Orthodox, Protestant—continue to affirm the evocative language codified in the ancient creed of Nicea.

Who is this Man?

We believe in one Lord, Jesus Christ,
the only Son of God,
eternally begotten of the Father,
God from God, Light from Light,
true God from true God,
begotten, not made,
of one Being with the Father.

Through Him all things were made.
For us and for our salvation
He came down from heaven:

by the power of the Holy Spirit
He became incarnate from the Virgin Mary,
and was made man.
For our sake He was crucified under Pontius Pilate;
He suffered death and was buried.
On the third day He rose again
in accordance with the Scriptures;
He ascended into heaven
and is seated at the right hand of the Father.
He will come again in glory to judge the living and the dead,
and His kingdom will have no end.

A Scripture project to rediscover the story of the Bible

As retold, edited, and illustrated by a gifted team
of writers, scholars, poets, pastors, and storytellers

A New Way to Process Ideas

Chris Seay's vision for The Voice goes back 15 years to his early attempts to celebrate the beauty and truth of the biblical narrative. As western culture moved into what is now referred to as postmodernism, Chris struggled with a deep desire to preach the whole story of God. Much like the Hebrews at the time of the New Testament, emerging generations today connect with story rather than isolated facts. Too often, preaching is reduced to articulating truth statements somehow hidden in a complex, powerful, and redemptive story. Jesus taught through parables and metaphors;

modern Christians have attempted to translate His teaching into a system of irrefutable fact statements and something seems to be getting lost in the translation.

Hence, a group of writers, poets, scholars, pastors, and storytellers have committed to work together to bring the Scriptures to life in a way that celebrates both beauty and truth. The result is a retelling of the Scriptures: The Voice, not of words, but of meaning and experience.

The Timeless Narrative

The Voice is a fresh expression of the timeless narrative known as the Bible. Stories that were told to emerging generations of God's goodness by their grandparents and tribal leaders were recorded and assembled to form the Christian Scriptures. Too often the passion, grit, humor, and beauty has been lost in the translation process. The Voice seeks to recapture what was lost.

From these early explorations by Chris and others has come The Voice: a Scripture project to rediscover the story of the Bible. World Publishing and Ecclesia Bible Society have joined together to stimulate unique creative experiences and to develop Scripture products and resources to foster spiritual growth and theological exploration out of a heart for the mission of the church and worship of God.

Traditional Translations

Putting the Bible into the language of modern readers has too often been a painstaking process of correlating the biblical languages to the English vernacular. The Bible is filled with passages intended to inspire, captivate, and depict beauty. The old school of translation most often fails at attempts to communicate beauty, poetry, and story. The Voice is a collage of compelling narratives, poetry, song, truth, and wisdom. The Voice will call you to enter into the whole story of God with your heart, soul, and mind.

A New Retelling

One way to describe this approach is to say that it is a "soul connection," not just a "mind translation." But "translation" is not the right word. It is really the retelling of the story. The "retelling" involves work of translation and paraphrase, but mostly entering into the story of the Scriptures and recreating the event for our culture and time. It celebrates the role of scholars, but it also values the role of writers, poets, songwriters, and artists. Instead of a translation born strictly of academia, teams of scholars partner with a writer to blend the mood and voice of the original author with an accurate rendering of words of the text in English.

The Voice is unique in that it represents collaboration among scholars, writers, musicians, and other artists. Its goal is to create the finest tools to help believers experience the joy and wonder of God's revelation. In this time of great transition within the church, we are seeking to give gifted individuals opportunities to craft a variety of products and experiences: a retelling of the Scriptures, worship music, a worship film festival, biblical art, worship conferences, gatherings of creative thinkers, a website for individuals and churches to share biblical resources, and books derived from exploration during the work.

The heart of each product within The Voice project is the sense of events of the Bible coming alive. To accomplish the objectives of the project and to facilitate the various products envisioned within the project, the Bible text is being encountered. We trust that this retelling will be a helpful contribution to a fresh engagement with Scripture. The Bible is the greatest story ever told, but it often doesn't read like it. The Voice brings the biblical narratives to life and reads more like a great novel than the traditional versions of the Bible that are seldom opened in contemporary culture.

Readable and Enjoyable

A careful process is followed to assure that the spiritual, emotional, and artistic goals of the project are met. First, the retelling of the Bible has been designed to be readable and enjoyable by emphasizing the narrative nature of Scripture. Beyond being simply a set of accurately rendered individual words, phrases, and sentences, we have asked our teams to craft the biblical texts with sensitivity to the flow of the unfolding story. We asked them to see themselves not only as guardians of the sacred text, but also as storytellers, because we believe that the Bible has always been intended to be heard as the sacred story of the people of God. We assigned each literary unit (for example, the writings of John or Paul) to a team that included a skilled writer and biblical and theological scholars, seeking to achieve a mixture of scholarly expertise and literary skill.

Personal and Diverse

Second, as a consequence of this team approach, The Voice is both personal and diverse. God used about forty human instruments to communicate his message, and each one has a unique voice or literary style. Standard translations tend to flatten these individual styles so that each book reads more or less like the others—with a kind of impersonal textbook-style prose. Some translations and paraphrases have paid more attention to literary style—but again, the literary style of one writer, no matter how gifted, can unintentionally obscure the diversity of the original voices. To address these problems, we asked our teams to try to feel and convey the diverse literary styles of the original authors.

Faithful

Third, we have taken care that The Voice is faithful and that it avoids prejudice. Anyone who has worked with translation and paraphrase knows that there is no such thing as a completely unbiased or objective restatement. So, while we do not pretend to be purely objective, we asked our teams to seek to be as faithful as possible to the biblical message as they understood it together. In addition, as we partnered biblical scholars and theologians with our writers, we intentionally built teams that did not share any single theological tradition. Their diversity has helped each of them not to be trapped within his or her own individual preconceptions, resulting in a faithful and fresh rendering of the Bible.

Stimulating

Fourth, we have worked hard to make The Voice both stimulating and creative. As we engaged the biblical text, we realized again and again that certain terms have conventional associations for modern readers that would not have been present for the original readers—and that the original readers would have been struck by certain things that remain invisible or opaque to modern readers. Even more, we realized that modern readers from different religious or cultural traditions would hear the same words differently.

For example, when Roman Catholic or Eastern Orthodox readers encounter the word "baptism," a very different set of meanings and associations come to mind than those that would arise in the minds of Baptist or Pentecostal readers. And a secular person encountering the text would have still different associations. The situation is made even more complex when we realize that none of these associations may resemble the ones that would have come to mind when John invited Jewish peasants and Pharisees into the water of the Jordan River in the months before Jesus began His public ministry. It is far harder than most people realize to help today's readers recapture the original impact of a single word like baptism.

In light of this challenge we decided, whenever possible, to select words that would stimulate fresh thinking rather than reinforce unexamined assumptions. We want the next generation of Bible readers—whatever their background—to have the best opportunity possible to hear God's message the way the first generation of Bible readers heard it.

Transformative

Finally, we desire that this retelling of the Bible will be useful and transformative. It is all too common in many of our Protestant churches to have only a few verses of biblical text read in a service, and then that selection too often becomes a jumping-off point for a sermon that is at best peripherally related to, much less rooted in, the Bible itself. The goal of The Voice is to promote the public reading of longer sections of Scripture—followed by thoughtful engagement with the biblical narrative in its richness and fullness and dramatic flow. We believe the Bible itself—in all its diversity, energy, and dynamism—is the message and not merely the jumping-off point.

The various creations of the project bring creative application of commentary and interpretive tools. These are clearly indicated and separated from the Bible text that is drawn directly from traditional sources. Along with the creative resources and fresh expressions of God's Word, the reader has the benefit of centuries of biblical research applied dynamically to our rapidly changing culture.

The products underway in The Voice include dynamic and interactive presentations of the critical passages of the life of Jesus and the early church, recorded musical presentations of Scripture originally used in worship or uniquely structured for worship, artwork commissioned from young artists, dramatized audio presentations from the Gospels and the Old Testament historical books, film commentary on our society using the words of Scripture, and exploration of the voice of each human author of the Bible.

The Team

The team writing The Voice brings unprecedented gifts to this unique project. An award-winning fiction writer, an acclaimed poet, a pastor renowned for using art and narrative in his preaching and teaching, Greek and Hebrew authorities, and biblical scholars are all coming together to capture the beauty and diversity of God's Word.

Writers

The writers for The Voice who have contributed to **The Last Eyewitness: the final week** are:

- **Chris Seay**—church planter, pastor, president of Ecclesia Bible Society, and internationally acclaimed speaker. His previous books include *The Gospel Reloaded* (co-authored with Greg Garrett), *The Gospel According to Tony Soprano*, and *Faith of My Fathers* (with his father and grandfather).
- **David Capes**—Chair of the Department of Christianity and Philosophy at Houston Baptist University. He has written several books including *The Footsteps of Jesus in the Holy Land*.
- **Brian McLaren**—Internationally known speaker and author of ten books including *A New Kind of Christian* and *A Generous Orthodoxy*.
- **Lauren Winner**—Lecturer at Duke University Divinity School, and author of *Girl Meets God* and *Real Sex*.
- **Greg Garrett**—Professor of film and writing at Baylor University and author of several books including *Free Bird* and *Cycling*.

Other writers for The Voice that are working on other products include:

- **Phyllis Tickle**, D.Hum., author/icon

- Tim Keel, pastor/author
- Phuc Luu, chaplain and adjunct instructor
- Don Chaffer, singer/songwriter, poet
- Charlie Hall, singer/songwriter
- Christian McCabe, pastor/artist
- Amanda Haley, biblical archaeologist
- Chad Karger, counselor/author, pastor
- Allison Smythe, poet
- Justin Hyde, pastor/author
- Kelly Hall, editor/poet
- Jonathan Hal Reynolds, poet
- Dieter Zander, author/pastor

Scholars

Biblical and theological scholars for The Voice include:

- David Capes, Ph.D., department chair/professor
- Alan Culpepper, Ph.D., dean/professor
- Creig Marlowe, Ph.D., dean/professor
- Peter H. Davids, Ph.D., pastor/professor
- Jack Wisdom, J.D., lawyer
- Nancy de Claissé Walford, Ph.D., professor
- Darrell L. Bock, Ph.D., professor
- Dave Garber, Ph.D., professor
- Joseph Blair, Th.D., professor
- Kenneth L. Waters, Sr., Ph.D., professor
- Peter Rhea Jones, Sr., Ph.D, pastor/professor
- Troy Miller, Ph.D., professor
- Felisi Sorgwe, Ph.D., pastor/professor

Most of the initial product offerings will include creative commentary. The purpose is to further the narrative message. The conversion of historical insight and exegetical study into a narrative setting engages the reader more completely in the biblical event. To distinguish the additional material from the Bible text, the notes are always set apart by boxes or unique type font. The user has all the information necessary to differentiate the Scriptures from the ancillary material. At the same time the reader is challenged to truly empathize with the characters of the Scriptures and be open to an emotional and spiritual encounter with the text.

Artists

Art and images will be incorporated into each book that will provide a visual reference, source of meditation, and convey the splendor of God's story that cannot be captured in words. Illustrations by **Rob Pepper**—accomplished British artist—bring beauty, dignity, and life to *The Last Eyewitness: the final week*. Drawing with a technique he has termed the *conscious reflex drawing* method, Rob deliberately does not look at the paper while drawing. Instead he focuses solely on the object. This technique keeps the hand consciously responding in the moment, rather then being influenced by the mind/eye interplay. This gives the drawings a fresh perspective and liberates the work from optical preconceptions and visual judgments. Through *conscious reflex drawing* Pepper captures the real essence of a situation and moment.

When applied to the Jesus story an inspiring reimagining takes place. Created from viewing preexisting artworks in London churches and museums, these illustrations were drawn at times during services (with messages and hymns), sometimes alone with only candlelight, and other times among the crowds of the National Gallery. The images are imbued with a potent "now" that recognizes the history, art, and inspiration of the church from over 2,000 years. Yet they also bring an immediacy of representation to the life of the Christ.

The drawings undertaken for The Voice project are a part of a wider series of artworks known as the Doxology series. These use *conscious reflex drawings* as conceptual tools to create dialogue about the nature of an experiential relationship with the Divine.

Carrying the Cross
The National Gallery, London
A broken Jesus carries the cross to Golgotha.

John the Apostle
The British Museum, London
Taken from twelfth century enamel in the British Library. The Gospel, depicted in John's hand, is embellished with gold, illustrating the importance this book is to have on the evolution and beliefs of civilizations over the next 2,000 years.

St. John the Evangelist
The National Gallery, London
St. John is often depicted with an eagle representing his role as the Evangelist and a symbol of inspiration. The gold chalice is emblematic of faith in following The Way foretold by Jesus.

Jesus Washing the Disciples' Feet
The National Gallery, London by Tintoretto
Kneeling before Peter, Jesus, dressed in an apron which has replaced the golden robe that has been set aside, washes his feet as the rest of the disciples look on. A gold curtain hides the watching Judas, and the highlighted flames of the fire are used as a metaphor to show the shining Light of the World.

The Lord's Supper
St. George's Church, Hanover Square, London by William Kent
(Doxology drawing)

Seated at the table as the disciples listen, Jesus teaches about what is to come. The tabletop, highlighted in gold, focuses on the invitation to all, welcomed irrespective of race, gender, or creed to the table. The gold light symbolizes the light of Christ.

The Vine and Branches
Tree By The River Otter, by Devon

Rob returned to his childhood home to draw his favorite tree for this image. It grows with its branches overhanging the River Otter in Devon, UK. This setting reflects the intimate and organic relationship that followers of Jesus share on The Way.

Jesus Teaching
The National Gallery, London by Poussin

This drawing focuses on Jesus the Teacher. Emphasis is placed on the cup and the bread that represent both the body and blood of Christ.

Agony
St. Mary le Strand (Doxology drawing)

The *Agony* was drawn shortly after the bombings in London in July 2005. For Rob it contains an important expression of grief for the city. Yet through this anguish it has become a symbolic beacon of hope. Jesus kneels, praying, with the gold placed on the cross showing the inevitability of his death. An angel offers a divine cup providing faith and belief to help deal with the assurance that dying eventually will come to us all.

Pilate Presents Jesus
The National Gallery, London

Pontius Pilate holds the golden sword of justice and presents Jesus to the crowds. Jesus' face shows the realization of his inevitable fate, while Pilate seems shocked at the crowd's judgment.

Beaten
The National Gallery, London
Ambiguously, the golden rope both binds and supports the whipped and beaten Jesus. The golden shadow illustrates that even though Jesus may not be physically present, His love and compassion exists when people are in their most dark and beaten places.

Crown Of Thorns
The National Gallery, London
Bruised, battered, and beaten, Jesus stands in pain as he is adorned with a crown of thorns.

Crucifixion
St. Paul's Cathedral, London (Doxology drawing)
Drawn during evensong at St. Paul's Cathedral in the center of London. The *Crucifixion* drawing shows the cross of Jesus transformed into a beautiful tree, which is decorated with golden leaves. As the crops are being harvested bystanders look on in shock and grief.

Death Of Jesus
The Harvard Chapel, Southwark Cathedral, London Bridge, London (Doxology drawing)
A stylized gold cross stands tall as the dead Jesus is lowered into the arms of His lamenting, loving followers.

The Resurrected Jesus Appears to Mary Magdalene
The National Gallery, London
Appearing first to Mary Magdalene, the resurrected Jesus stands outside His tomb. As with the *Crucifixion* drawing, the tree is emblazoned in gold symbolizing the tree of life.

Jesus Appears to the Disciples
The National Gallery, London
Jesus stands amidst the disciples as Thomas places his finger in the wound that convinces him that Christ has risen from the dead.

Jesus Appears To Peter
The Victoria & Albert Museum, London by Raphael
Christ appears to Peter and gives him the keys of heaven. He gestures towards a flock of sheep, telling Peter to feed and take care of them.

The Ascension
St. James Garlickhythe, Garlick Hill, London (Doxology drawing)
The Ascension moves away from the narrative drawings that make up most of the Jesus series to an increasingly flowing minimal form. The more fluid abstract style represents Jesus returning to the "One that sent Him." The spirit of how this happens is left open to be decided by the viewer.

Musicians

The passages meant for use in worship are being set to music with a number of music albums planned. The first CD is a truly amazing collection of artists and sounds containing 13 original songs inspired by selected Psalms from The Voice. The recording itself was an experience of collaboration and worship. A large studio was selected to allow up to 20 musicians to perform live, creating a truly dynamic sound. Most of the featured artists participated in many of the songs making a diverse and rich sound. The spirit of the retelling of the story found in The Voice comes through in this unique collection of songs in a variety of styles and moods. The featured artists are:

- Derek Webb
- The Robbie Seay Band
- Jami Smith
- Sandra McCracken
- Seth Woods
- Sara Groves
- Jill Phillips
- Waterdeep

hearthevoice.com

A vital part of The Voice is our website www.hearthevoice.com. Tyndall Wakeham, a minister of technology and culture with Ecclesia in Houston and Blackpulp Designs is creating a truly exciting place to share ideas and experience the latest in Scripture translation, musical arrangements, worship ideas, and exploration of the emerging trends in the future church. Come to www.hearthevoice.com and meet, see, hear, and experience The Voice in our times.

A Final Word

These times of transition in which we find ourselves have been described in many ways. It is widely agreed that both our secular and religious cultures—from the most liberal to the most conservative—have been deeply affected by a mindset labeled "modern," and we now are grappling with the appearance of a new cultural ethos often called postmodern. This transition has many dimensions: philosophical, artistic, technological, social, moral, economic, political, and theological. It is no surprise that in times of transition like these, fresh attention needs to be paid to how we translate, study, understand, teach, apply, and proclaim the vital message of the Scriptures.

During this unique time in the life of the church of Christ there seems to be a change as to how we as the body of believers worship, fellowship, and communicate the truths of the gospel. The Voice appears at the point of impact where the modern church, with its tradition and stability, collides with the developing church of the future. This is our effort to help work through these changes and to focus attention on God's word to us. In reality, The Voice is the product of a community of believers seeking to bring alive the story of the Bible. The goal is to reinvigorate followers of Christ with the Scriptures. Together we all are weaving together our talents to retell the story and create tools to use with the narrative communication of the Bible. Together we are rediscovering the story of the Bible.

Scripture Index